HIS
VISION

Cavin O'Ferral

ISBN 978-1-63630-847-0 (Paperback)
ISBN 978-1-63630-848-7 (Digital)

Covenant Books, Inc.
11661 Hwy 707
Murrells Inlet, SC 29576
www.covenantbooks.com

First and foremost, and even before that, this book is dedicated to God, my Father, and to my *two* big brothers, Jesus Christ and the Holy Spirit, who gave me His vision for the Crips and Bloods to become Christians.

I also dedicate this book to the Crips and Bloods throughout the United States of America. Please take heed to what God is saying to you all. He loves you all of the time. No matter what you have done in your past, God forgives you and wants you to give your lives to Him.

His Vision is also dedicated to all gangbangers throughout the world. God wants every last one of you to cast your cares upon Him for He cares for you. No matter what you think of Him or have been told of Him, He loves you more than anyone on this earth could ever love you.

I also dedicate *His Vision* to all of the churches and communities in gangbanging neighborhoods. There's a message in there for you.

I also dedicate *His Vision* to my wife and kids. Thank you for your patience and love that you are showing me throughout my incarceration. I am sorry that I took so long to allow God to use me. If I would have allowed God to use me a long time ago, I would not have had to be locked up away from y'all in order to hear His voice.

ACKNOWLEDGMENTS

I would like to thank God for trusting me with this important work of His. I am humbled that He would use me to reach out to all of the gangbangers that would have an ear to hear and eyes to see what He wants for them.

I also thank Terry Moses, Quin Epps, Nitty, Young Dub, MD, and Timothy Ross for allowing me to use their names as characters in this book. God thanks you gentlemen too.

Terry Moses, God has used you to encourage me throughout the writing of *His Vision*. I am forever grateful for that. Timothy Ross, thank you for allowing God to use you to give me advice about writing the appendix for *His Vision*. Quin Epps, thank you for proof-reading *His Vision* and letting me know that you feel the Holy Spirit in this awesome work of God.

Uncle Smitty, what can I say? I love you and thank you for teaching me how to write short stories. I could never fade your writing skills, yet you still encouraged me to keep on keeping on.

Poppa Rick Stevenson, thank you for adopting me as your spiritual son and for your encouragement and for supplying me with several books of stamps to send out query letters to all of those potential publishers. You were the main reason that the music group Tower of Power had such great success as you were their lead singer on all of their original hits. Since they do not seem to be giving you your props, now God has put you in the real Tower of Power, the kingdom of heaven. And in God's eternity, you will always be "Still A Young Man."

I also thank my cellmate Todd Cerra and my ex-cellmate Marlan Simpson for their encouragement and confirming the Lord's work. Ed Cerra, my cellmate's father, thank you for making yourself available to help me get copies and addresses to Christian publishers and also for stamps too. You are a godsend.

A special thanks goes out to Me-Ma and the whole Meeks family for accepting me as one of their own. Me-Ma, God used you to tell me to write this book. Thank you for being obedient to His call on your life.

I also thank my sister, Queen Ayo "Christ," for proofreading this awesome work of God and helping me get it out to the masses. I love your enthusiasm. God is not done with us, sis. He is going to use us to move many more mountains out of people's lives. I also thank Brother Greg Pruitt for allowing the Holy Spirit to use you to help me with ideas that He was bouncing off you, which was actually confirming what He was and is doing with me. Thank you, my brother in Christ.

Last but certainly not least, I like to thank my son, Lil' Kevin, who resides in heaven with God, the Father, and Jesus Christ. It was his passing that God used to teach me the power of forgiveness. I'll be in heaven with you, son, and I am bringing all of these Crips and Bloods with me. Amen!

Grace and peace to you all. Amen!

PROLOGUE

Big Lou, Money Mike, Jim Jones, Con Man, O. G. Van, Rick-Rock, Mad Man, and Killa Martin (all gang names) were kicking it on Altadena Dr. in Altadena, California, where they were always getting high off in marijuana and drinking Old English 800 beer in the back of some apartment.

Around at the same time, down in Pasadena, California, MD, D-Rock, Lil' John, Deuce Rock, One Punch, Bam-Bam, and a few other youngster were also kicking back in the projects called King's Manor. They were also getting high off in marijuana and Old English 800 beer.

The higher both groups became, the more Satan was getting control over them. The group of youths in Altadena decided to call themselves Crips, and their gang name would be Altadena Block Crips (ABC 123) while the group of youths in Pasadena decided to become Bloods and called themselves the Pasadena Denver Lane Blood Gang (PDL).

While the Altadena Block Crips represented blue rags and the word *cuz*, the Pasadena Denver Lane Blood Gang represented red rays and the word *blood*. They became the worst of enemies.

Narrator

These two groups of youths don't even know each other, and here they are in two different parts of a city being made as each other's worst enemies. Ready to actually kill each other because of a word that each group has chosen to use (*cuz* and *blood*) and because of some colors that represent their gang colors—blue for the Crips and red for the Bloods. Only the spirit of Satan and his demons could have brought about that evil assignment. The Spirit of the Lord is much stronger than Satan's, and it will be the power of forgiveness that will ultimately win the souls of those youths. Thus, we have *His Vision*.

> And they may recover themselves out of the snare of the devil, who are taken captive by him at his will. (2 Timothy 2:26)

Amen!

1
CHAPTER

Scene jumped to 1984

Big Lou, Money Mike, Jim Jones, O. G. Van, and a few of the other Altadena Block Crips were participating in their favorite pastime—smoking weed, drinking Old English 800 beer, and shooting dice. While they were doing that in the back of the projects, their homeboys were slanging rock cocaine to the cars that were coming in and out of the spot (apartments).

While all of that was normally going on, a car came into the projects and slowly rode through to the back where the dice game was taking place. As the car got closer to the group in the back, a red rag was put outside of the passenger window. One of the dope dealers saw it, but it was too late to warn his homeboys. The car pulled up on the dice shooters and started firing a gun on them relentlessly. The dice shooters scrambled to get out of firing range. As they were fleeing, O. G. Van was returning fire for he was the only one with a gun on him. None of O. G. Van's bullets hit any of the Bloods, but one of his bullets went through an apartment window and killed a five-year-old girl.

The killing was blamed on the Bloods, and the Altadena sheriffs never solved the shooting. The Crips knew that it was their bullet that killed the little girl. O. G. Van was emotionally hurt about shooting that little girl, but not so hurt that he would turn himself in.

The Crips just left the blame on the Bloods, and that lie was a reason enough to go and try to kill one or more of the Bloods, plus the drive-by the Bloods just did on them was also a reason enough to go smoke one or more of them.

As the Bloods sped away from the drive-by shooting, they were not aware that someone got shot but was hoping to have at least a shot on one of the Crips. They dropped each other at their respective homes, where they were staying with their mothers (there were no fathers in their homes nor in the Crips' homes). (All of the Crips and Bloods were from the ages of sixteen to twenty-five years of age.) As each one of the Bloods shut their homes' doors behind them, their mothers, then and only then, got off on their knees, praying that God would bring their child home safely.

Meanwhile, the Crips (Big Lou, Money Mike, O. G. Van, Con Man, Rick-Rock, Jim Jones, Lil' Kevin, and Rocket) were about to retaliate against the Bloods for that drive-by. Big Lou and Rick-Rock were the only ones with cars, so they split up in two cars loaded of fours. In Big Lou's car were O. G Van, Jim Jones, and Lil' Kevin while Rick-Rock had Money Mike, Con Man, and Rocket. O. G. Van still had his gun on him that he just killed that little girl with, and Money Mike went and got his gun.

They got drunk off on some Bacardi rum and Old English 800 beer, and about one in the morning, they drove down to the Bloods' hood and rode around until they found a group of them hanging out. The group of Bloods they found were doing the same thing that they were doing when they were fired upon—shooting dice and getting high off in marijuana and Old English 800. Their homeboys that did the drive-by on the Crips did not warn them about what they had done earlier. So this group of Bloods were not the ones that shot the Crips. The Crips did not know what the Bloods that shot them looked like. Not that it mattered—they were looking for any Bloods that they could find.

As they road up on the group of Bloods, O. G. Van stuck his gun out of the passenger's side window, but one of the Bloods saw it and warned his homeboys, and they scattered to their feet and ran as he fired upon them. The other car loaded of Crips also started firing their gun. By this time, one of the Bloods got his gun out and started firing back at the Crips as he was running away. None of the Crips' bullets hit the Bloods, and none of the Bloods' bullets hit the Crips, but one of the Bloods' bullets did go through an apartment window and hit and killed a five-year-old boy.

That murder was blamed on the Crips, just as the Crips blamed their murder on the Bloods. The Crips and the Bloods did not know that they were being misused by Satan.

The two cars loaded of Crips drove off and dropped each other off at their homes. As each Crip entered their homes, where they were staying with their mothers, each mother heard the door closed behind their sons, then and only then did they get off on their knees from praying that God would bring their child home safely.

The next morning, the Crips met on the block to talk about what happened the night before. As they were about to start talking, an undercover cop's car came riding up real slow, as if they were about to do a drive-by, like they were trying to get some type of reaction out of them. The Crips knew that they were the sheriffs, so they just stood there, mean-mugging them.

The car stopped right in front of the Crips. The officers got out of their car and told the Crips to get up against the wall and searched them, expecting to find at least one weapon, thinking that they would be strapped just in case the Bloods came back to shoot at them. Jim Jones was praying that O. G. Van did not have that gun on him that killed that little girl.

There were no weapons or drugs found on them, so they were told to sit down on the curb.

One of the sheriffs said, "We know that the Bloods did a drive-by on you, Crips, last night and that a stray bullet hit and killed a little girl, and we know that you, Crips, retaliated last night and killed a little boy with a stray bullet."

No one was talking, so they did not have anyone to arrest. They just knew or felt that it was one of them.

At the same time, the Bloods were going through the same scrutiny down in their hood by the Pasadena police that the Crips were going through by the Altadena sheriffs.

After the Altadena sheriffs left the Crips, the gang went and got a newspaper to read. That was in the paper, about the shootings, and that is when they found out just like the sheriffs said—a little boy was killed. They did not know that it was not their bullet that hit and killed the little boy, just as the Bloods did not know that it was not their bullet that hit and killed the little girl in the Crips' hood. For after the Pasadena police left, the Bloods too went and got a newspaper, and that's when they found out that one of their bullets was being blamed for killing a little girl.

Now both sets of gangbangers were feeling guilty about what they had done, but not guilty enough to put away their guns. As a matter of fact, their guilt just made them madder at their enemies.

Narrator

The devil was really playing with the gangbangers' minds. Instead of their guilt making them repent and do what was right, Satan was using it more so to make them hate each other even more.

2
CHAPTER

The mothers of the eight Crips that started that gang in Altadena got together at one of their homes after they had read the newspaper. They all arrived at the same time, and as they formed a circle, unrehearsed, in the living room, tears rolled down their faces. One by one, they threw a copy of their newspaper in the middle of their circle onto the floor. As each mother threw their paper onto the floor, they grabbed each other's hands (but no one would touch each other while the other was holding the newspaper). As the last mother threw in her paper, they were in a perfect circle. With heads bowed, they started praying in tongues.

The mothers never called each other or set up that prayer vigil. They were just moved upon by the Spirit of the Lord, and they were obedient to the call.

The mothers of the Bloods were moved upon to do the same thing. They (about eight mothers) went to one of their homes. One by one, they all pulled up at a mother's home with newspaper, and they formed a circle. Each one dropped their newspaper in the middle of the circle. They grabbed each other's hands (but none of them would touch each other while the other was holding the newspaper) and started praying in tongues. No one called each other to set that prayer vigil either. They were just moved upon by the Spirit of the Lord.

After both sets of parents prayed (unbeknownst that they were both doing and going through the same thing), they never spoke to each other. They just all left knowing that God would be dealing with this whole situation.

Narrator

The mothers would not hold hands with each other until they each dropped the newspaper because they were in the Spirit of the Lord, which means that they were not in agreement with what the newspaper had to say. Once they threw the papers out of their hands, they came into agreement with what the Holy Spirit was praying in and through them in tongues. That's why they grabbed each other after releasing those newspapers.

> Again I say unto you, That if two of you shall agree on earth as touching anything that they shall ask, it shall be done for them of My Father which is in heaven. (Matthew 18:19)

*****

After the Crips read the newspaper, they called a meeting with all of their homeboys and homegirls to talk about the killing of the little boy that they had supposedly killed in the Bloods' hood. At the meeting, they all agreed to let things die down before they do anything else against the Bloods because the sheriffs were hot trying to find out who did the actual shooting. The Bloods also called a meeting to say that they too were going to lay low because the police were snooping around their hood too. Then both hoods would decide their next course of action.

The brother of the little girl that the Crips killed (but was blamed on the Bloods) was thirteen years old, and his name was Smooth. He was walking around the Crips' hood, looking like something was on his mind.

Jim Jones walked up to him and asked, "Why aren't you at the park with the rest of the kids?"

Smooth answered, "When I hear the other kids playing and laughing, it reminds me of my little sister, and it makes me sad." Then he asked Jim Jones, "Do you know which one of those Bloods killed my little sister?"

Jim Jones knew exactly who killed the kid's little sister, and it was not the Bloods. But he could not tell the kid what he knew, so he continued the lie and told him, "No, I do not know which one of those Bloods killed your little sister, but we are trying to find out."

Smooth said, "When you find out, will you let me know who he is so I can talk to him?"

Jim Jones asked the kid, "What would you say to him?"

The kid shocked Jim Jones by saying, "I want to let him know that my momma forgives him so she will not be sad anymore."

Jim Jones said, "If we do not kill him first."

The kid looked at Jim Jones with tears in his eyes and said, "If you kill him, then his momma would be feeling like my momma." Then the kid asked, "When is it going to stop?"

Jim Jones said, "I do not know when it is going to stop." Then Jim Jones told the kid, "Go home, kid."

Smooth said, "Before I do, let me tell you one more thing, and that is this. It could all stop right here, right now, with y'all the Crips and Bloods."

That kid was ahead of his time. As Smooth was walking away, he looked back at Jim Jones and said, "Do not forget that we want to talk to the shooter so my momma and I can tell him that we do forgive him."

Jim Jones said, "I'll see what I can do." Jim Jones just shook his head as he watched the kid left.

Meanwhile, down in the Bloods' hood, D-Rock and MD were walking through their hood when they saw the sister of the little boy that was killed by them (but was blamed on the Crips). She was twelve years old, and her name was Samantha. She walked up to MD and D-Rock and asked them if they had a minute. They said sure.

Before she spoke, MD (the shooter of her little brother) asked her, "How is your mother doing?"

Samantha said, "We are doing fine, but we are more concerned about the shooter of my little brother."

MD asked her, "What do you mean by that?"

She said, "My mother and I want to let him know that we forgive him."

MD could not even think like that, so he was at lost for words. All he could think of was to say, "It's getting dark out here. Can we walk you home?"

She said, "Please do."

As they were approaching Samantha's apartment, the door swung open, and Samantha's mother came out onto the porch. Samantha ran up to her mother, hugged her, and told her (not knowing that they were the actual shooters themselves), "These are the guys that are looking for the guy that shot my little brother."

The mother asked them, "What are you going to do with him once you find him?"

MD said, "It would be taken care of."

She said, "Don't y'all realize that this cannot go on and on? If it does, all this world would have is a bunch of grieving mothers. You boys find out who it is and bring him to me, and I will have a talk with him."

MD and D-Rock looked at each other and shook their heads, not knowing what to make out of this. MD said, "We will see what we can do."

The mother said, "You guys ain't that hard core, or you would not have walked my daughter home. There is some goodness in you all."

Narrator

When the sister and the brother of the slain children were talking to the Crips and Bloods, the demons in the atmosphere fled away from over the gangbangers.

3
CHAPTER

The mothers of the Bloods got together a few days after the prayer vigil. They had decided to go talk to the mother of the little boy that was killed in their neighborhood. They knocked on her door, and her twelve-year-old daughter, Samantha, answered the door.

They asked if her mother was in, and Samantha asked in return, "Yes, may I ask who are they?"

All the while, the mothers and Samantha were smiling for they knew that they were at a divine appointment. They told Samantha that they were the mothers of all these boys running around terrorizing the neighborhood.

Samantha said, "Please come in and have a seat while I go and get my mother."

There were eight mothers that came. They sat down and waited for Samantha to come back with her mother, who was in her room praying for God to use her in this gangbanging community.

The moment her daughter, Samantha, knocked on her room's door, she (the mother) was ending her prayer with, "In Jesus's name, amen!" So as she was ending her prayer, God was already answering it. The mother opened her bedroom door and asked her daughter on what she needed.

Samantha said, "Some of those gangbangers' mothers are here to see you."

The mother looked up toward the heaven and said, "Thank You, Father God."

She couldn't see him, but there was an angel right above her, shaking his head, as if to say, "Yes, God hears your prayers."

She went into her living room and was blessed to see eight women in her home, knowing that they were sent as an answer to her prayer.

One of the mothers spoke up and said, "We are so sorry to be here bothering you, but we were moved upon by the Spirit of the Lord to come and see how you are holding up."

Another mother said, with tears in her eyes, "We also wanted to apologize for our sons' behavior in this community."

The slain child's mother said to the eight mothers, "Please, listen to what I am about to say to you all very carefully for what I am about to say to you is not me speaking but the Lord, the Great I Am, in me. I can also see God in you all as well."

As she was speaking, she could see the tears coming down the beautiful faces of the eight mothers in her living room. They just knew that they were about to be spoken to by the Lord Himself.

The lone mother continued, "Everyone calls me Mommu, and your names are?"

The eight visiting mothers all said their names, and Mommu continued, "You, beautiful ladies, do not have to apologize to me about your sons' behavior. This battle that we are all in is not with flesh and blood, but it's a spiritual warfare. Your sons are being influenced by demons, and we must pray those demons off on our kids. Do not worry about me grieving my son's passing for I have given him over to the Lord. My son is in heaven with our Lord. How can I be mad about that? I'll be with them both real soon for all eternity. The more important thing is that we make sure that the rest of our boys make it to heaven too. That also goes for the Crips and Bloods.

"We must pray for God to lead us to their mothers so we can all stand in agreement together for it states in Matthew 18:19–20, 'If two of you shall agree on earth as touching anything that they shall ask, it shall be done by My Father which is in Heaven. For where two or three are gathered in My name, there I Am in the midst of them.' Amen! We must not let the enemy have our kids."

One of the eight mothers said that they all stood in agreement with her and thanked her for her humility and forgiveness, and then she said, "We came here to comfort you, yet you have comforted us and also given us some understanding about this situation, but more importantly, you have given us hope and even some direction. We thank you and stand in full agreement with you."

Another one of the mothers said that she had the police chaplain's number and that she would call him and see if he could hook them up with the mothers of the Crips.

Narrator

God was giving them ideas and ways to bring about their attack on the enemy once they all came into an agreement.

*****

Meanwhile, the mothers of the Crips (about eight of them) got together and went over to the house of the mother whose five-year-old daughter got killed (everyone called her Me-Ma).

They knocked on her door, and Me-Ma answered. Once she saw eight ladies at her door, she knew they were the mothers of those youngsters in their projects. They introduced themselves, and Me-Ma invited them in.

As they entered the apartment, they could literally feel the Holy Spirit holding them. Me-Ma had been playing an anointed Gospel song by Juanita Bynum called "Morning Glory." The eight mothers looked into Me-Ma's eyes, and they knew that she knew exactly who they were the parents of. So Me-Ma raised her hands up to them and said, "Please listen to me very carefully."

Just as the mothers of the Bloods knew, so did the mothers of the Crips knew that they were about to be spoken to by God Himself through this anointed sister.

Me-Ma continued, "I can feel that you all wish to apologize to me for the behavior of these youngsters around here, but your apologies are not needed because they did not wrong me or my family. It was, and is, the enemy, Satan, that is attacking us and our children. The enemy is not the Crips and Bloods. No, that is just a smoke screen that the real enemy is blinding everyone with. Our warfare is not with flesh and blood or to each other neither is the warfare between our youths that are killing each other. As long as Satan has them fighting each other, they will stay blinded to the truth—that he's the enemy, not them to each other. We have to renew their minds through fasting and prayer."

As she was speaking, the music of Juanita Bynum was playing in the background of her apartment, just as it was in the apartment where the Bloods' mothers were touched.

The Spirit of the Lord was moving through all of the mothers, and one of them spoke up and suggested that they would try to get in touch with the mothers of the Bloods so that they can all get together to stand in agreement with the fasting and praying that was being spoken of there in Me-Ma's apartment.

So they (the mothers of the Crips and Me-Ma) all grabbed hands and stood in a perfect circle and prayed for God to show them the way to get in touch with the mothers of the Bloods. As they were praying, Me-Ma was moved upon by the Lord to get in touch with the chaplain of the sheriff's station who had given her his card just in case she needed someone to talk to.

*****

O. G. Van and Jim Jones were kicking it on the block, drinking some Old English 800 beer and smoking weed, when O. G. Van (who was the shooter of the little girl) said that he kept having dreams of hearing gunshots going off really loudly then he would wake up.

Jim Jones told him that it would go away soon.

O. G. Van said, "I'll be glad when it does, and I will never fire my gun again unless I can see exactly where the bullet is going into." As he was talking, tears were coming down his face.

Right at that time, they saw all of the mothers coming out of the apartment of the slain child. It seemed as if the mother of the little girl was comforting them. O. G. Van and Jim Jones looked at each other and eased out of their sights.

4
CHAPTER

Down in the Bloods' hood, MD (the shooter of the little boy) was talking to his homeboy D-Rock and was telling him how he was having dreams of just hearing gunshots going off in his head when he sleeps. He also made a vow to make sure that he sees where the bullets would go when he fires from his gun. The devil was using their guilty feelings to harden their hearts.

The chaplain of the Pasadena police station came to the Bloods' hood late, one night, where he thought he would find some or most of them hanging out. There were about sixteen of them kicking it when he pulled. He asked if he could talk to them, and they all just stood there without responding. So he took that as a yes.

He said, "I just wanted to let y'all know that you are not being looked at as the shooters of that little boy that the Crips shot the other night."

The Bloods knew that the Crips did not shoot that little boy, but they're sure not to tell the police chaplain that. The chaplain continued, "If any of you need someone to talk to, I will be here for you."

He tried to pass out his calling card, but no one took them. He then said, "I'm not here as a cop to lock you up but as a man of God that wants to help you."

MD spoke up, "When you say that you are here not as a cop but as a man of God, what does that exactly mean? Are you a cop or not?"

The chaplain asked, "Would that make a difference?"

D-Rock said, "Being that we do not trust cops, yeah, it does make a difference."

The chaplain said, "God will always be first in my life and in my decisions, whether I am wearing a badge or not. So the answer to your question is yes, I am a cop, but first and foremost, I am a Christian. I only came here to see if any of you wanted someone to talk to, to let y'all know I'll be here for you as a friend or a Christian. You will never have to worry about me as a cop."

As he turned to leave, he laid down twelve of his calling cards on the ground. None of the Bloods would pick any of them up.

The Crips were chilling in their hood when an undercover cop car pulled up on them. As the car came to a stop, they all just stood up knowing that it was a cop, but they never saw this one before, and he did not have a uniform on. As they stood up, O. G. Van was in the back of everyone, pulling out his gun to hide it behind the wall that they were kicking it on. The unknown cop saw what O. G. Van was doing, but he acted like he did not see it.

The cop asked, "Do you gentlemen have a minute?"

The Crips did not respond, so he took that as sign of them saying yes. He said, "I am the chaplain of the Altadena sheriff's station, and I heard about the Bloods killing that little girl here in your hood. I just wanted to let y'all know that if you wanted anyone to talk to, I am willing to be here for y'all, as a man of God, that is."

The Crips knew that it was not the Bloods that killed the little girl, but their own bullet did that damage, but they were not gonna tell about that to the cop.

As the chaplain was talking, he was trying to pass out his calling card, but no one would take them. He said, "I understand that you all are not taking my calling card or not even talking to me, but I am not here as a cop but as a man of God. If I were here as a cop, I would be putting cuffs on someone for that gun behind that wall that y'all are kicking on."

Instinctively, they looked at O. G Van, as if to say, "You are slipping, Cuz."

Jim Jones tried to get the chaplain's attention off on the gun by asking, "What does a man of God want with us?"

The chaplain said, "I am only here to let y'all know that everyone is not your enemies, and God moved upon me to come and see if any of you needed someone to talk to. I would never trip on y'all as a cop would, but I would always be here for y'all to talk to."

Jim Jones said, "We appreciate that, but we are cool."

The chaplain said, "I understand, and I will just leave these calling cards of mine here, on the ground, just in case any of y'all want one." He laid down his calling cards and then got in his car and left.

O. G. Van picked up his gun and said, "That was too close, Cuz."

Jim Jones asked him, "Is that the same gun the little girl was killed with?"

O. G. Van said, "Yeah, Cuz."

Jim Jones said, "We have to get rid of that thing, Cuz."

O. G. Van said, "As soon as I get another one, but I am not about to be caught without a strap."

Jim Jones told him, "If you get caught by the police with that strap, they are going to tie you to that little girl's killing."

O. G. Van said, "The police think that the Bloods did that, not us."

Jim Jones responded, "That gun will tell the police something different."

O. G. Van just shook his head, like oh well. Jim Jones understood him too.

*****

On a Sunday morning, all of the mothers of the Bloods went to their local church and all of the mothers of the Crips went to their local church as well. Before the services were about to start, in the church in Pasadena (where the mothers of the Bloods were), the pastor of the church told his congregation that he had a special anointed speaker that wanted to say something to them. It was Mommu, the mother of the little boy that was killed in the drive-by by the Crips.

She said, "My son has passed on to heaven. Praise God, Almighty, amen, amen."

The whole congregation said, "Amen."

Before she said another word, she saw the mothers of the Bloods were coming down to the front where she was at, and when they got down to the podium, they turned around to face the congregation, tears were rolling down their faces.

Mommu continued her message. "These ladies are the mothers of the gangbangers in our community. They need our prayers for God to use this situation to bring their children out of the enemy's hands. My son is in heaven with God, the Father, and Jesus Christ, our Lord, who was taken away the sting of death. Now we all want what's best for our children, right? With that being said, there is no better place for my son to be then, right there with Jesus Christ and God. I mean that with all of my heart."

As she said those profound words, her twelve-year-old daughter came down to the front of the pulpit and held hands with the crying mothers of the Bloods.

Mommu continued, "We, the church of this community, need to all get together and stand in agreement in prayer that God would soften the hearts of our children to hear and receive His love through us. Most of our kids do not have fathers in their lives, so we need/ must commend them to God, and He will be their Father. We must believe in our prayers, and God will move on our behalf. We must also get in touch with the mothers of those Crips to stand in agreement with us in prayer for their boys and girls too. This warfare that we are in is not with flesh and blood, but it is a spiritual warfare against principalities, against powers, against rulers of the darkness of this world, against spiritual wickedness in high places. With that being said, I propose for us to walk seven laps around our projects. Anyone willing to participate as our brothers and sisters did in the Bible in the book of Joshua, we will take seven days to walk one lap a day, and on the seventh day, we will walk seven laps. Anyone willing to be involved, please see me after the service here today. Thank you for your time."

The congregation all stood up and clapped their hands for a good minute or so.

The head pastor of the church grabbed Mommu's hands and beckoned for the mothers of the Bloods to come up on the stage. They all went up on the stage as asked. They all turned and faced the congregation, and the pastor said, "Please remain standing as I pray for continued guidance in this battle for the mothers, sons, daughters, and the community."

After the service, everyone in the church signed on to walk seven laps around the projects where the Bloods hang out. So it was decided to start the seven-day journey right then and there. Once a day for seven days, the choir would lead the way in a song as the rest of the church followed. That was on a Sunday, and they would all meet at the church every day after that until the victory laps were over that coming Saturday.

Meanwhile, the church in the Crips' hood just had a regular service with some special prayer for Me-Ma and her remaining son.

The Crips were trying to figure out how to come up with some more guns for all of their homeboys. So they invested in some crack cocaine to sell on the street and trade some for guns. Once the crack-heads heard that the Crips were trading crack for guns, they started doing burglaries looking for guns. Within four days, the Crips came up with twelve guns and some knives and brass knuckles.

Narrator

The devil tried to step up his attack because he knew what the churches were doing. They were fighting him in the spiritual realm with God's armor.

*****

The Bloods were also trying to come up on some more guns. They too started trading drugs for guns, and they were doing burglaries and also had some crackheads doing burglaries to find guns and other weapons. In five days, they too came up with about twelve guns and some knives.

The Crips called a meeting on the block, and about thirty of them showed up. At the meeting, Jim Jones and O. G. Van passed out the guns and assigned them to the cars of Big Lou, Money Mike, Rick-Rock, and Lil' Kevin. Each driver had three shooters. The plan was to go down into the Bloods' hood and catch them slipping and fire on them in three back-to-back cars without any of the Crips getting shot—like a shock-and-awe operation.

The Bloods were also having a meeting, setting up the same type of an attack on the Crips. MD and D-Rock called the meeting, and about forty or fifty Bloods showed up. They had many more gang members than the Crips. They passed out their weapons and assigned three shooters to four cars, just as the Crips did, and they also planned the same type of drive-bys.

Narrator

Notice how the attacks were so similar. That's because they were being set up by the same spirit of Satan. The youths were being misused by Satan.

*****

The pastor of the church where the mothers of the Bloods attend called the pastor of the church where the mothers of the Crips attend and told him what happened at this church—how they all planned to take back their youth and their hood. There was a video made of the service, and he wanted to send a copy of it to his church.

"Of course," the other pastor said, and he also told him that his church stood in agreement with their church.

A copy of the video was delivered up to the church in Altadena. After the pastor viewed the video of the mother testifying how God had completely delivered them and had revealed to them a way to take back their youths and their community, he took the video out of the VCR and sat there holding it in his hands. He could feel the anointing through the video that was on the mother whom God was speaking through. So the pastor prayed for God to give him direction to get his congregation in agreement with that movement that was taking place in the church where the mothers of the Bloods go to.

As he was praying, God moved on him to show the video to his congregation as soon as possible. So he called Me-Ma (the mother of the slain little girl in the Crips' hood) and asked her if he could come over and show her a special video made by the church where the mothers of the Bloods go. She agreed, and he went over to her place with the video. Before he gave her the video to put in her VCR, he asked her to put her hands on it as he prayed for complete understanding and agreement by her and his congregation.

After he prayed, Me-Ma said, "I can already feel His anointing on me and that video." She put the video in and sat down to watch it.

As she saw and heard where the mother was going, she knew that her spirit was bearing witness with hers. As she was watching the video, the pastor saw a glow came over Me-Ma, which confirmed to him that the Spirit of the Lord was heavy upon her. Just as the part of the video where the speaker's daughter came down the aisle to hold hands with the mothers of the Bloods, the pastor could only stare at Me-Ma's feet as tears came down his face for he felt the presence of the Lord as his spirit was bearing witness with the girl on the video. He knew exactly what she was feeling for he was feeling it too.

After watching the video, Me-Ma told the pastor, "We must implement this movement within our church and community. I feel exactly the same way as the mother on this video feels and would like to meet her."

The pastor was pleased to hear her response and said that he was pretty sure that he could hook her up with the speaker on the video. He also told her that he wanted to make sure that she was in full agreement before he showed the video to the congregation. So he had his church's staff called all of the congregation to hold a special service in two days so that they could get this movement implemented immediately and be in agreement with the church in Pasadena.

5
CHAPTER

So the congregation would see the video in two days instead of waiting 'til Sunday, which was six days away. By the time the Altadena church saw the video, the church in Pasadena had already marched two laps around their projects. They were immediately obedient to the call of the Lord. The first day was that Sunday that the Lord gave them the direction. The choir took the lead in full robes singing "We Shall Overcome" the first day and "He Is Here" the second day. The deacons fell in line behind the choir reading Joshua 6:1–19, then the congregation came in behind the pastor. They were in twos, about a hundred people deep. It was such a beautiful sight to see—the sight of a walking church, not just a talking church.

Everything just fell right into place for them. You could literally see God. People stopped in their cars, trying to figure out what was going on. When they heard the choir singing and saw the deacons reading the Bible and the pastor praying and the congregation following in twos (a roll of one hundred people in twos), they came to the correct conclusion that these people were having church in the hood.

While the Pasadena church was circling the projects in the Bloods' hood, the Crips were talking about making sure that they would kill one or more of the Bloods that they would fire upon.

Neither the Bloods nor the Crips knew that they were being protected by the Spirit of the Lord because of the prayers and the circling of their hoods by the churches in their neighborhoods. The Bloods were already inside a bubble of protection by the beginning of the circling of the church in their hood. The Bloods were inside that protective spiritual circle (unknowingly inside of it), planning the same type of murderous attack against the Crips, just as the Crips were planning to do to them.

The Altadena gang task force and the Pasadena gang task force were working together, knowing that some type of retaliation will be continuing back and forth between the Crips and the Bloods. So they were riding around in both hoods, pulling over gang members and anyone that looked like a gang member. That alone was enough to slow both gangs down from getting in their cars and doing their planned drive-bys.

Narrator

The Spirit of the Lord was allowing the sheriff's and the police's presence to slow down the planned attacks so that the circling of both hoods could be completed before anyone else got killed. The police and sheriffs did not mind the Crips and the Bloods killing each other, but it was the killing of those two kids that had them out in full force.

*****

The church in Altadena, where the mothers of the Crips go, all got a phone call for a special service, which was to be held two days after the pastor saw the video with Me-Ma (the mother of the slain girl).

Everyone received the phone call about the special service and were more than willing to show up and watch the video. They all filed into the church. It was about 150–200 people that showed up. The sheriff chaplain also received a phone call from the pastor himself, and he showed up too.

After everyone was seated, the pastor walked over to the podium with Me-Ma. The pastor spoke to the congregation, "You all are about to see a God-anointed and God-appointed movement to reclaim/take back our youths and our communities from the enemy. The Crips and the Bloods are not the enemy. They are being attacked by the real enemy—Satan. They are under a spiritual attack, and they do not know it. But we know it, and it is our job to take the battle to the enemy.

"The Crips and the Bloods do not know how to fight the enemy, but we do. So that's what we are going to do. We are going to put on God's spiritual armor and defeat the enemy for our youth and our community. Jesus Christ fought the good fight for us before we gave Him our lives. He fought the good fight for us before we were born into this world. So just as He did it for us, we must do it for our youth and neighborhood."

Before he showed the video, he asked Me-Ma if she had anything to say. She said, "Yes, there is."

He introduced her to the congregation. Some people knew her, and some did not. Me-Ma grabbed the mic and said, "My daughter was sent to heaven in that drive-by shooting that took place in our projects. I just want all of you to know that I have already seen the video, and I stand in full agreement with the movement that God has put upon their church. If the person who shot my child came up to me, I would forgive him and then let him know that he is being controlled by the enemy. We must let him know that he is being controlled by Satan and let them know how to defeat him. So please, watch this video with a spiritual heart."

The pastor led them in prayer and then showed them the video. As the video was playing, they could hear people saying, "Praise God. Hallelujah."

Meanwhile, the Crips were checking in with each other, making sure that none of them got caught slipping, riding around with one of the guns that they were going to use. None of them got caught, but they all agreed that they should lay low for a week or so 'til the sheriffs stop sweating them.

Narrator

That week of laying low would give the churches enough time to finish their reclaiming laps around the projects. Please know that there is no such thing as a coincidence.

*****

The Bloods were also checking in with each other to make sure that none of them got caught slipping with any of their guns. None of them got caught slipping, and they too agreed to lay low for a week or so to let things die down.

Since the Crips and the Bloods were laying low, waiting for the cops to back off, they both were moved upon to give a barbecue.

The Bloods would figure out where to have theirs, just as the Crips would figure out where to have theirs. There was a real big park called Brookside, and it's connected to the Pasadena Rose Bowl. Both sets of gangs were moved upon to have their barbecues at Brookside park at the same time. So while the Crips were making their spread on one side of the park, so were the Bloods making their spread on the other side of the park. Neither knew that the other was there. The park was big enough that they could actually be there at the same time and not know it.

Both groups had a few of their homegirls with them and a few kids too. Both groups had alcohol and marijuana along with some loud music, and everyone was chilling and feeling good. None of the Crips or Bloods brought guns because of the heat that was being put upon them by the police and the sheriffs. There was a restroom right in the middle of both respective areas. The men had no problem relieving themselves in the bushes, but the women had to go to the restroom to take care of their business.

The music was playing loud, and the kids were running around playing tag. The Crips were drinking beer and getting high off on some real good weed they had.

The Bloods were also getting high off on some weed they had, and they were also drinking beer and just chilling while the food was being barbecued.

Narrator

It was Satan that moved upon both groups to have a barbecue at the same time, at the same place. It was Satan's plan to get them away from their hoods because there was a spiritual movement and power in their hoods that had already defeated Satan. That defeat came with the death and burial and resurrection of Jesus Christ. That's the spiritual power that was taking over the Crips' and the Bloods' hood by the obedience of the churches walking laps around the projects, praising God, *war*shiping/*word*shiping, and reading *scrip*ture over their hoods.

So Satan thought that if he could get them away from their hoods, then he could have them get off on each other; and thus, they would be too mad at each other to allow anything or anyone stop them from trying to kill each other. But Satan did not count on them not having any weapons. That was God's plan—not to allow them to have any guns—for God was still protecting them from the enemy, and it was also God's way of answering the churches' prayers. God was blessing/honoring the churches' obedience of walking around the projects for seven days.

*****

Some of the Bloods' women had to go to the restroom, so MD and D-Rock walked them over there, and two of the kids went as well. The kids were six and seven years old (a boy and a girl). When they got to the restroom, the woman went in and left the kids out there with MD and D-Rock.

Now about the same time, some of the women with the Crips had to go to the restroom, so Jim Jones and O. G. Van walked them over there. They also had two kids with them. The kids were five and seven years old (a boy and a girl).

Narrator

Just as the fathers of the Crips and Bloods were not in their lives, neither were the fathers of those four kids that were with the Crips and Bloods. The trend was continuing.

*****

As Jim Jones and O. G. Van were approaching the restroom, they saw MD and D-Rock dressed in red clothing (their gang colors).

MD and D-Rock had not turned around yet to see who were coming up behind them. The kids from both groups saw each other and immediately ran up to each other to play, as if they had known each other all of their lives, yet they never have met.

When D-Rock noticed the kids running away from the area toward the other kids, he then turned around, and that's when he saw Jim Jones and O. G. Van coming their way with two women and two kids. D-Rock tapped MD, and MD turned around to see what was happening. The women with Jim Jones and O. G. Van realized what was happening when they looked up and saw the sets of men mad-dogging each other, as they were walking toward each other to get off with their fists since they did not have any weapons. The ladies that were walking with Jim Jones and O. G. Van jumped in between both groups, and one of them was talking to the Crips while one of them was talking to the Bloods, pleading them to think about those kids over there playing with each other.

As the two women with O. G. Van and Jim Jones were trying to speak some sense into both the Crips and Bloods, the other two women that came with the Bloods walked out of the restroom and saw what was happening and heard what the other women were saying to the Crips and the Bloods about watching out for the children. They ran and grabbed all four of the kids and tried to keep their attention away from the fracas.

Once the kids were secured, one of the women that came with the Bloods walked over to where they were tripping at and told her homeboys (the Bloods) that they need to stop being so selfish and think about those kids and the women that were with them. She went on to say, "We already lost two kids due to some misdirected bullets."

That's all O. G. Van and MD needed to hear for they were the shooters of those two kids (even though they did not know that about each other).

Jim Jones and D-Rock also felt it because they also knew that their homeboys, MD and O. G. Van, were the shooters. So they all just stopped in their tracks. That statement stopped everything that was about to take place. Even the kids stopped playing.

O. G. Van told Jim Jones, "Let's go, Cuz."

MD looked at D-Rock and told him, "Let's get out of here, Blood."

Before both groups left, the women looked at each other with true concern for each other. The kids asked if they could keep playing. Both set of women spoke at the same time, "Not right now."

One of the kids asked, "Why not? Ain't that what parks are for?"

One of the kids asked Jim Jones, "What did those guys do to you?"

Right then, it dawned on Jim Jones that those guys did not do anything to him.

The kid said, "Y'all should try playing with each other like us because it's fun."

Narrator

Out of the mouths of babes—when one of those kids asked what did they do to them, it awoke the Spirit of the Lord in Jim Jones. Then he remembered how the kids ran when they saw each other and just started playing even though they never had seen each other 'til that day. But the grown-ups were ready to run up on each other and start fighting. In the kids' actions and the grown-ups' actions, you could see the difference between God and Satan.

*****

As Jim Jones and O. G. Van and the women with the kids were walking back to their area, the women spoke up and told them to make sure that they would take them home before they would do something stupid. O. G. Van and Jim Jones could not even talk because they were still tripping off from the remembrance of those kids being shot. MD and D-Rock and the women that they were with were tripping off from the same thing that the Crips were tripping on.

When Jim Jones and the rest made it back to their area, one of the Crips walked up to them and said, "Cuz, y'all look like y'all seen a ghost or something."

All Jim Jones could say was, "Cuz, we got to get out of here."

The women told them that there were some Bloods over at the restroom and that they were about to get off on each other, but they were reminded of the kids.

The Crips all came over to hear what had happened. They started asking questions like, "Were they strapped?" "Where are they now?" "How many of them are there?"

While they were asking those questions, O. G. Van was just standing there like he was in a daze, so Jim Jones started answering them.

He said, "There were two of them that we saw. Those two probably were not strapped. As far as how many they are altogether, I do not know. As far as why we did not get off on them, the women that we both were with stood between us and reminded us of the kids that were with us and the kids that were recently killed."

The moment Jim Jones stopped talking, O. G. Van had tears in his eyes and said, "I ain't killing no more kids, Cuz. Someone take me back to the hood."

As MD and D-Rock and the women with the children returned to their area, their homeboys and homegirls could tell that something happened, so they all ran up to them, asking what was up.

MD said, "We ran into some *crabs* [a disrespectful term for Crips] over at the restroom."

A few of the Bloods were ready to go back to the restroom area and look for the Crips, but MD spoke up and said, "They have kids with them and females too."

One of the Bloods said, "We ain't after the kids or the females. We want those crabs."

The females that were with MD and D-Rock said, "We all agreed not to trip because of the kids and us, females, being with y'all."

MD said, "Check this, our Blood. I'm not gonna be responsible for another child being killed or hurt."

Another Blood said, "We ain't strapped, so all we are going to do is fistfight."

MD said, "But we do not know if they are strapped."

That statement wiped out all arguments. So the Bloods and the Crips all packed up and left the park.

As they got to the exit, they both were at the red light in four car loads a piece, side by side, waiting for the light to turn green so they could go their separate ways. They were just mad-dogging each other, not knowing if the other was strapped or not. They were both throwing up gang signs and waving their blue and red rags (gang colors) at each other. It was about two o'clock in the afternoon when the Crips and the Bloods left Brookside park.

When the Crips got back to their hood, they saw a really long line of people coming around the corner. So the Crips went to the entrance of their projects, where they had to wait for the long line of people to pass by. It just so happened that O. G. Van and Jim Jones were in the front car watching the procession go by.

O. G. Van (the shooter of the little girl) looked at Jim Jones and said, "This walk has something to do with us, Cuz."

O. G. Van was in the front seat while Jim Jones was in the back seat. They watched the choir go by first singing "He Is Here." Then they saw the neighborhood church pastor went by praying in tongues. Then they saw the deacons of the church walked by reading Joshua 6. Then they saw the whole congregation walked by in twos. The first two people that they saw were the mother (Me-Ma) of the slain little girl and the chaplain of the sheriff's station. They were holding hands like everyone else in line. The last two that they saw in the line were the brother of the slain little girl. He was holding hands with an elderly member of the church. As the kids passed by, he looked at O. G. Van and bowed his head, as if to say, "God bless you."

O. G. Van looked at Jim Jones and said, "Cuz, what's all this?"

Jim Jones said, "It's some type of church movement."

Narrator

God's timing is always perfect. Notice how He timed the Crips' and the Bloods' departure from the park to coincide with the marches around the projects. Satan tried to have them beat each other sense-less, but God separated them and ran them back to His safe haven— the reclaimed projects.

6
CHAPTER

As the four car loads of Bloods approached their hood, they also saw a long procession of churchgoers coming around the corner. MD and D-Rock were in the front car, and as they came to the entrance gate, they made a conscious decision to wait before going through the line. For some unknown reason to them, they were attracted to it. It was the light of God that was attracting them.

The first part of the line that they saw was the choir singing "He Is Here." Then they saw the neighborhood church pastor praying in tongues. Then they saw the deacons reading Joshua 6. Then they saw the congregation walking in twos in about as long as a line that they ever did see. The first two church members they saw were the mother (Mommu) of the slain little boy, walking next to the police chaplain. The last two people they saw were the sister of the slain little boy. She was walking with an elderly church member. As the girl was walking by, she looked at MD and bowed her head, as if to say, "God bless you."

MD looked at D-Rock and said, "Did you feel that, Blood?"

D-Rock said, "Yeah, Blood, I felt that."

Now the church in the Bloods' hood only had three more days of circling the projects. As the Crips and the Bloods drove up into their respective projects, they could feel something (the Holy Spirit) that seemed to make everything look and feel a little brighter. As the Crips pulled up into the back of the projects, they all got out of their cars and looked around and saw all of the neighborhood kids out playing like never before.

For some reason, their parents were not worried about them getting hit by a stray bullet or them seeing drugs being sold right in front of them. It then dawned on Jim Jones that they have been holding these kids hostage by not allowing them to enjoy their own neighborhood.

The Crips had a lot of extra food because they left the barbecue a little earlier then they had planned. So instead of selling some drugs, they started passing out barbecue hamburgers, hot dogs, chips, and sodas. They were giving crack addicts food instead of drugs. The Crips all said that it felt good to be doing something right for a change.

As the church completed its daily lap around the projects, the kids' parents all came to their doors to call their children in. They were moved upon by the Holy Spirit at the same time that the church ended their lap.

By the time the last kid made it to his apartment, O. G. Van told Jim Jones, "It's crazy how all of the kids have mysteriously disappeared once we got back in the hood."

Jim Jones said, "Yeah, Cuz, that is a trip. Let's go see if those church people are still walking around our hood."

As Jim Jones and O. G. Van got to the front of the projects, they could see the last of the church group turning around the corner, heading back to their church. The little boy (the brother of the slain little girl) turned and looked at Jim Jones and O. G. Van and waved his hand for them to come.

They shook their heads no.

Meanwhile, as the Bloods pulled into their projects, they also saw all of the neighborhood kids out playing like never before. For some reason, the hood looked a lot brighter. The Bloods also had a lot of food left over from the barbecue. So instead of selling crack, they were looking at the crackheads with some concern and started feeding them the extra food that they had.

MD and D-Rock were drawn back to the front of the projects. As they reached the front, they saw the end of the church's procession going back to the church.

The last person that they saw was the little girl that they had walked home (the sister of the slain boy). She looked back at them and waved for them to come along.

They shook their heads no. As MD and D-Rock walked back into the projects, they noticed all of the kids going into their respective apartments as the parents all seemed to come to their doors as the church was leaving.

Narrator

The Spirit of the Lord moved upon the parents of the kids to allow their kids out to play. He also moved upon them to bring them in. God also allowed the Crips and the Bloods to be aware that the kids were out playing like never before. God also made sure that the Crips and the Bloods realized that the kids were going in all of a sudden. With each lap that the church walked, the projects became a little brighter, as if a light was shining just over the projects (not the surrounding area).

*****

The Altadena sheriff chaplain called a meeting with the gang task force of their department. This gang task force pretty much knew all of the Altadena Block Crips by name. The gang task force members were about fifteen deep, and they wore street clothes, as undercover cops would. Sometimes they would wear face masks and bulletproof vests so they could look more menacing than the Crips and Bloods.

Narrator

The same spirit of evilness that was working on the Crips and the Bloods was also working on the task force officers. They considered themselves a gang in their own right. Thus, that is/was their mentality when the chaplain was talking to them.

*****

The chaplain came into the room where he was holding the meeting, and he was struck by how hard the task force officers were looking. He felt like he had walked into a room full of gangbangers. The chaplain told the officers that he had been with the neighborhood church in the Altadena Block Crips' hood and that God had a major anointing on that church to take back that neighborhood and those Crips from the enemy.

One of the task force officers spoke up and said, "We are willing and able to remove those gangbanging thugs from that neighborhood." The rest of the officers all agreed.

The chaplain told them something that they were not ready for. He said, "The enemy is not the Crips and the Bloods themselves, but it is Satan and his demons that are misusing those youths."

The officers could not understand the things of the Spirit because they were not of the Spirit themselves. So the chaplain asked them to watch the video of the church movement (copies were passed out to whoever wanted one in the church) in a church service that had the mother of the slain little boy that the Crips allegedly killed. They all agreed to watch it.

As the task force was watching the video of the mother speaking about forgiveness and taking their neighborhood back from the enemy, they were all looking befuddled. A few of them even walked out of the video room in disgust that someone could even mention the word *forgiveness* in that circumstance. After the video was over, the chaplain asked if there were any questions.

The two officers that walked out came back in to voice their disgust. One of them asked, "Are the police still needed since God has touched that mother in such a special way and His touch has spread through her to their neighborhood church?"

The chaplain said, "You should continue to do your job as needed, and if you notice any changes in the Crips and their hood, I would like to know."

After the task force officers left the room, the chaplain felt a little disturbed by their response. So he prayed right there in the video room that God would soften their hearts.

Narrator

The chaplain felt more comfortable talking to the Crips than he did talking to the task force officers. The officers seemed more harder to reach than the gangbangers.

*****

The chaplain in the Pasadena police department (in the Bloods' neighborhood) asked their task force officers to watch the video as well. They agreed to watch it and basically had the same response that of the Altadena task force officers had. They even asked the chaplain, and he said, "Of course, you are needed. Plus, the church in the Crips' community feels the same way as this church on the video feels."

The task force officers just shook their heads in disgust and left the room.

The chaplain prayed for their hearts to be softened. He also felt that it was easier talking to the Bloods than the officers.

One of the Pasadena task force officers called the Altadena task force officers and asked if they had seen that video made at the church in the Bloods' hood—walking laps and talking about forgiveness. The Altadena task force officer said that they had seen it and that they were not in agreement with it and also told the Pasadena task force officer that the church in the Crips' hood were doing the same thing.

Both officers let each other know that they did not agree with the chaplains of their departments, acting like it's all good. The officers were disturbed by the fact that the mothers of the slain children were the ones pushing this movement of forgiveness toward the killers of their children.

So the officers agreed to meet so they could put all of their resources together to make sure that the killers of those kids won't be getting any type of reprieve or forgiveness.

The chaplains from both departments called each other and both had concerns about the task force officers' responses. They both agreed that the officers had a lot of hatred in their hearts for the Crips and the Bloods. It was like the officers were a gang within themselves. So the chaplains prayed right there over the phone that the officers' hearts would be softened and that their hatred of the Crips and the Bloods would disappear as they would see the power of the churches' obedience to take back their youths and their neighborhood. After they prayed, they were moved upon by the Spirit of the Lord to go talk to the Crips and the Bloods and ask them how do they see the gang task force in their respective hoods.

The Altadena sheriff chaplain went to the Crips' hood after he had lunch. So it was around one in the afternoon when he got there. He parked down the street and walked up into their hood. As he walked inside the front gate of the projects, he saw a few old men just kicking back, drinking liquor.

One of the Crips walked to the back of the projects to warn his homeboys that a cop was there. The chaplain had no fear in him, so he followed the youth to the back, knowing that he was warning them that he was coming.

Just as the Crip got to his homeboys to tell them that that cop chaplain was coming, they told him that they know because he was right behind him.

There was about nine Crips there drinking Old English 800 and smoking weed. None of the Crips had guns on them, but they had them strategically placed under cars and in bushes, right there where they were at.

The chaplain asked, "Can I speak to you guys about the gang task force officers and how they treat y'all?"

Jim Jones spoke up, "Why do you keep coming around here like we are cool with you or something?"

The chaplain said, "Because I care for you guys, and I know who the real enemy is." When the chaplain said he knew who the real enemy was, the Crips thought he was talking about the task force officers because that's who he was there asking about. Some of the Crips actually thought he was talking about the Bloods too.

One of the Crips, Mad Man, said, "The task force are always riding around harassing us."

The chaplain realized that the Crips thought he was talking about the officers being the enemy. So he just let them keep that assumption so they would keep talking since that's who he was there to talk about anyway.

Money Mike said, "We would just be kicking back or walking to the store then a car of task force officers would roll up on us, as if they were gangbangers themselves, jump out of their cars with guns drawn, telling us to get on the ground. They would search us and get mad when they did not find anything, so they would start kicking us and talking crazy to us."

Another Crip, Big Lou, said, "They think that they are scaring us, but all they are really doing is pissing us off and making us want to do something to them. They even talk bad to our mothers."

The chaplain asked, "What do you mean they talk bad to your mothers?"

Big Lou said, "Our mothers would see us getting jacked up by the officers, and they would actually point their guns at our mothers and tell them to shut up and say, 'If you were raising them right, they would not be out here terrorizing people.'"

The chaplain did not want to believe that the officers would actually point their guns at the mothers, but after seeing the officers' response to the video, he figured that it was probably true.

Meanwhile, the chaplain of the Pasadena police department went to talk to the Bloods about the task force officers in their hood. As the chaplain approached their hood, one of the Bloods' lookouts saw him parking his car down the street. The spotter went to the back of the projects to warn his homeboys. They all put their guns in the bushes and under car tires around them.

When the chaplain came up on the Bloods, he could tell that they knew he was coming. The chaplain could also see one of the guns in the bushes that was not hidden very well. But he did not say anything about it right then. Instead, he asked, "What type of relationship do you have with the gang task force?"

D-Rock said, "We do not have a relationship with them."

MD said, "They act more like the enemy than the Crips do toward us."

D-Rock continued, "Yeah, they roll up on us with their guns drawn, talking crazy to us and even crazier to our mothers."

Another Blood said, "I would rather beat up or even kill a task force officer than I would a Crip."

The chaplain asked, "Do you all think that the Crips feel the same way about the task force officers in their hood?"

MD said, "Of course, they do. Their task force officers are more than likely to treat them the same way that we are treated in our hood."

The chaplain apologized for those officers' behavior and said that he would check into it for them. As he was leaving, he turned around and said, "Hide that gun a little better next time. Yet you wonder why those officers come with their guns drawn."

No one said anything. They just stood there looking at each other. Once the chaplain was out of sight, they all grabbed their guns.

D-Rock said, "I wonder why he did not trip on us about that gun?"

MD said, "*Be-blood* he wants us to trust him as a pastor and a friend instead of fearing him as a cop."

Narrator

Notice how the Blood gang member MD did not say "because." Instead, he said "be-blood." The word *cause* sounds too much like their enemies' favorite word *cuz/cause*.

*****

The Pasadena police chaplain called the Altadena sheriff chaplain and told him how his talk with the Bloods went. After hearing what the Bloods told the Pasadena chaplain, basically the same thing that the Crips told him, both chaplains agreed to go ask both churches to include those officers in their prayers. They also agreed to let the mothers of the slain children know the disturbing news that they found out about the officers in both hoods.

7

CHAPTER

Meanwhile, the Pasadena task force officers were riding around in the Bloods' hood, like predators themselves, seeking whom they may pick (devour) on. It dawned on them that every time (recently) they rolled up in the Bloods' hood, things seemed to be more brighter (the atmosphere) more so than it did outside of the projects. Like there was some kind of light that was turned on in a room, in a house. Even the Bloods were not hanging out like they used to. The officers wanted to talk to one of the Bloods and ask them about what was going on. Even as the officers left the projects, they noticed the difference of the brightness inside of the projects, as opposed to the darkness outside of the projects.

Up in Altadena, about nine Crips were walking to the store down the street from the projects. As they got about two houses away from the store, they saw a man beating up his girlfriend pretty badly. He was much older than the Crips but not much bigger.

Me-Ma (the mother of the slain little girl) was coming out of the store and saw the man beating the lady too. She also saw the Crips looking at the beating, and she could tell that they were mad about it.

O. G. Van told Jim Jones, "Let's stop this fool, Cuz."

Both of them walked over to where the man and the lady were. When they reached them, O. G. Van said, "That's enough, fool."

The old man looked at Jim Jones and O. G. Van and said, "Y'all better mind your own business."

O. G. Van told him, "Anything happening in our hood is our business."

By this time, the man was surrounded by all nine of the Crips. While the man was arguing with the Crips, Me-Ma ran over to the lady, who seemed to be a bit younger than the man. Me-Ma told her, "Come with me, baby."

The lady immediately followed Me-Ma. The man that was beating her saw that she was trying to leave, and he hollered for her to come back over to him. The lady stopped in her tracks, out of fear.

Once O. G. Van saw Me-Ma helping the same lady that he was trying to help, he felt obligated to help the lady.

Jim Jones noticed that O. G. Van's stance strengthen once he saw Me-Ma, so he told the man, "It would be best for you to get out of here, or you will be dealing with something more deadly than you could think of."

Me-Ma told the lady, "Just keep walking, baby, and do not look back at that mean man."

The lady kept walking with Me-Ma. They stopped right behind the Crips, and the Crips all started moving toward the man, and that's when the man realized that he should better get out of there.

He told the Crips, "All right, I'll leave."

O. G. Van told him, "We bet not to ever see you in our hood again. If we do, we will smash you."

*****

Down in the Bloods' hood, about seven of them were going to play some basketball at the Jackie Robinson Center Park. It's across the street from the projects. As they were crossing the street, they saw two men that they had never seen before, acting like they were waiting on a ride or something.

MD looked at D-Rock and asked him, "Have you ever seen them before?"

D-Rock said, "Nah, Blood."

Right at that moment, two ladies that they saw walking in the church procession around their hood earlier in the week were about to walk pass by the two men. By this time, all of the Bloods were watching the two men from down and across the street.

The two men did not see the Bloods, but the two elderly ladies did. As a matter of fact, the two ladies were talking to each other about the Bloods. One of them said, "Those are the boys that the Lord has us walking around these projects for."

Just as they said that, the two unknown men walked up on them. One of the men had a knife and told the women to hand over their purses. One of the ladies said, "You do not have to do this. Just ask for help, and we will give it to you."

One of the men said, "Just give us your purse, and no one will get hurt."

By this time, the Bloods had crept up from behind the two men. MD said, "Drop your knife, or you will be shot in the back of your head."

The two men were about to turn around, but D-Rock said, "Don't turn around."

MD said, "I am not going to repeat myself. Drop the knife, or die right now. The choice is yours."

The two men dropped their knife. As they did, the Bloods grabbed them and were about to whip on them, but the church ladies said, "Please don't whip on them for they do not know what they do. They are being misused by the enemy."

The two men started pleading with the Bloods not to kill them. It was then that the two robbers noticed that the Bloods did not have any guns on them, that they were buffed by the Bloods.

MD asked the elderly ladies, "What do you want to be done with them?"

The ladies said, "We forgive them. Just let them go, and we will be praying for them just like we are praying for you all."

One of the ladies asked the two robbers for their names so that they could pray for them by name. The other lady invited them all to come church on Sunday.

After the robbers gave the elderly ladies their names for prayer, the Bloods told them that if they were not on their way to the church, they bet not to catch them in their hood again.

One of the robbers asked the Bloods why did they make them think that they had guns when in fact, all of them could have just jumped on the two of them.

MD said, "We did not want to put these ladies in danger."

After the robbers left, the church ladies asked, "May we hug you boys?"

MD said, "Of course, you can."

As they were hugging the gang members, the gang task force were passing by, and when they saw the hugging going on, they just shook their heads in disbelief. The task force officers did not know that the Bloods had just prevented a robbery.

Narrator

Notice how the Bloods and the Crips were having their hearts softened by the Lord by being put in positions to do some protecting. The Lord was softening their hearts so they would be ready to receive the churches' reclamation.

*****

The church in the Crips' hood were continuing their mission of circling the walls of the projects. As they were about to start their walk, the pastor got everyone's attention and had them look at the difference between the brightness over the projects and the darkness or graying outside of the projects. The congregation was encouraged by the difference. The pastor was amazed by the difference himself. Everyone knew that God was honoring their obedience.

Before they started their lap around the projects, Me-Ma said, "I have a testimony to share. I witnessed myself the Crips came to the rescue of a woman that was being beaten by her boyfriend."

After hearing that, the whole congregation just started praising God right there on the spot.

At the same time, the church in the Bloods' hood was also about to continue their reclamation walk around the Bloods' projects when their pastor had them look at the difference of brightness over the projects and the grayness and darkness outside of the projects. That also encouraged their congregation. The elderly ladies that almost got robbed testified how the Bloods came to their rescue and stopped two men from robbing them. The church started praising God right there on the spot.

After both churches heard those testimonies of how the Crips and the Bloods were being used by God to protect the people, instead of hurting the people, it encouraged the congregation even more than seeing the difference of brightness over the projects as opposed to the darkness outside of them. The churches continued their marches around both hoods.

As the church in the Crips' hood were circling the projects, about halfway through the walk, the woman that was being beaten by her boyfriend and was saved by the Crips came looking for the lady that helped her, and she found her in the procession of walkers. When Me-Ma saw her, she reached out her hand to her and pulled her into the line with her. The lady just got in the line without saying a word.

As the church was finishing their lap around the projects, the Crips came out from the back of the projects. They came out because they heard the choir singing, and they noticed that it got a little brighter over their hood but not outside of their hood. When the Crips got to the front, they saw the church finishing their lap, and they wondered if that had anything to do with the way their hood, all of a sudden, got a little brighter.

The lady that they saved from being beat up looked at them as if she wanted to say something.

O. G. Van told Jim Jones, "That looks like the lady we saved the other day."

The church had finished their lap, and they only had two more laps to go in the next two days. As the rest of them kept on walking to their church, Me-Ma and the lady that the Crips helped out went over to the Crips. It was about nine of them standing there. The lady pointed at O. G. Van, and Me-Ma asked him if they could talk to him.

He was nervous, but he told them to go ahead and speak.

The lady had tears in her eyes as she said, "I just wanted to thank you personally for coming to my rescue."

O. G. Van said, "You do not have to cry, and you are more than welcomed." The he asked her, "Is that guy still messing with you?"

She said, "No, I have a restraining order on him." Then she asked O. G. Van, "Will you please escort me to the church on Sunday?"

He said, "I do not know about that." When he said that, he looked back at Jim Jones, as if to say, "Come get me out of this."

Me-Ma noticed how everyone seemed to look up to Jim Jones, so she approached him and asked, "Would you please escort an elderly lady to church?"

She was not talking about a date, or anything like that, for she was twice his age.

Jim Jones said, "I do not go to church."

Me-Ma said, "Look, you don't have to go into the church. Just escort us there and then come get us when it's over."

Then the lady that they saved from being beaten asked O. G. Van, "Can you at least do that for me?"

O. G. Van looked at Jim Jones and at the rest of his homeboys, and they all shook their heads yes.

So O. G. Van and Jim Jones agreed to escort the ladies to the church. Jim Jones asked Me-Ma, "How do we do this?"

Me-Ma and the lady smiled at each other as Me-Ma put her arm through Jim Jones's arm and said, "You can start by walking us to my apartment."

O. G. Van and Jim Jones told Me-Ma that they would do all that they were asked for.

8
CHAPTER

The church in the Bloods' hood was on their sixth day of circling the projects. The Bloods were in the projects chilling when a few of them realized that all of a sudden, things just got a little brighter than it was a moment ago. Then when they looked outside of the projects, it was not as bright. Then they heard the choir singing right outside of the projects. So they walked to the front of the projects just as the church was finishing their lap around the hood.

The two ladies that the Bloods stopped from being robbed saw them came out from the back. They walked up to the Bloods with the pastor of the church following them. When they got to where the Bloods were, they whispered into the pastor's ear as they pointed at the Bloods. The Bloods felt a calming Spirit came over them, and they couldn't move, so they just stood there in submission.

It was about 17 Bloods in the middle of about 250 church members.

MD asked, "What's going on?"

The pastor said, "We, as church, wish to thank you gentlemen for protecting our elderly sisters from being robbed."

MD said, "They already thank us."

The pastor said, "Yes, they did thank you personally, but now we wish to thank you as a church body because we are all one body at this church, and when you protected those two elderly sisters, you protected the whole church body. The deeper part of that is we, the church, are the body of Christ and He is the head, so you essentially protected the Son of God."

Right after the pastor said that, one of the elderly ladies said, "The Bible is true, and we read that Jesus said, 'If you done it for the least of these My brethren, you have done it for Me.'"

D-Rock said, "That's pretty deep."

The pastor said, "Yes, it is pretty deep because it's the truth."

MD said, "So what you are telling us is because we helped those elderly ladies, we have helped the whole church?"

The pastor said, "Not only the church but Jesus Christ Himself. That's what His Word says, and we believe Him to be the truth. As a matter of fact, it's not only the church thanking you but God Himself is also thanking you all through the church."

The Bloods actually seemed to be getting some understanding of what they were being told.

Narrator

As the church was talking to the Bloods, there were demons in the atmosphere trying to get back to the Bloods. But as the church surrounded the Bloods, angels entered the area, fighting off the demons. So as the church was talking to the Bloods, there was a spiritual warfare going on right above their heads, but the Bloods did not know it. Not even all of the church members knew it, but some of them did know and understand.

*****

The pastor asked the Bloods, "Have you guys noticed the light over your hood? Have you guys even noticed the darkness outside of your hood?"

They all shook their heads yes.

MD said, "What's up with that?"

The Holy Spirit moved upon the pastor to explain in detail what God had the church doing. So the pastor asked the Bloods to allow him five minutes of their time, and he would explain it all to them, and the Bloods all agreed to hear the pastor out. The Bloods did not know that agreeing to hear him out meant that they were about to be hit with some faith because faith comes by hearing and hearing by the Word of God.

Narrator

The Bloods did not know it, but when they agreed to hear the pastor, they were also entering in the spiritual law of agreement which says that if two or more agree on earth as touching anything that they shall ask, it shall be done of their Father which is in heaven. They agreed to hear the pastor, and the pastor was explaining Joshua 6. So unbeknownst to the Bloods, they were about to be moved upon with a measure of faith because they had agreed to hear the Word. Plus, they had already seen a miracle in the difference of the brightness over their hood as opposed to the darkness outside of their hood.

*****

The pastor started from the beginning of the church movement. He reminded the Bloods of the drive-by shooting that killed a little boy. The pastor did not know that he was speaking to the killer right there for it was the Bloods' bullet that hit and killed the little boy, not the Crips' bullet.

The pastor said, "The mother of that little boy, Mommu"— he pointed to her—"was moved with compassion for the boys that were being misused by the enemy. And she knows that you boys do not know that y'all are being misused by Satan. So she came to the church and gave us a testimony of how she forgives the person who killed her son and that she knows that the person who fired the gun does not know that he was being misused by Satan. So she has sacrificed her son to the Lord that she might win all of you gangbangers to the Lord."

As the pastor was speaking, Mommu walked right up beside to one of the Bloods with tears in her eyes, and she grabbed his hands, and the Bloods just held her hand tightly as tears ran down his face.

It was MD, the actual killer of her son, but she did not know it although God and MD knew it.

The pastor went on to say, "Satan meant for the death of the little boy for evil, but God meant it for good so that the Bloods and the Crips could live. The Lord has moved on the whole congregation to walk seven laps around the projects. In doing so, we will reclaim all of you gangbangers from the grasp of Satan and tear down the walls of Satan's hold on you all."

D-Rock asked, "What makes you think that will work here on us?"

The pastor said, "Because it worked in the Bible, and every Word in the Bible is alive and breathing. Plus, it's evident that it's already working."

D-Rock asked, "What do you mean that it's already working?"

The pastor said, "Just take a look at the darkness outside of your hood and now look at that light over your hood. Every time we walked around your hood in obedience to the Lord's call for us to do so, more and more angels [demons] of darkness left."

Then the pastor quoted this scripture from Luke 1:78–79, "Through the tender mercy of our God: whereby the day spring from on High hath visited us. To give light to them that sit in darkness, to guide our feet into the way of peace. Amen!"

MD spoke up and said, "That's why we came out to see what was going on with the brightness over our hood."

When everyone looked in the sky over the projects, they could still see the difference. The Bloods could not deny that God was in their midst.

The pastor said, "We will be back tomorrow to complete this blessed mission that God has appointed our church to do. You young men cannot deny that God is right here with us for that light that you see over your hood is God Himself honoring the church's obedience of His call. If any of you want to join this march around your hood, just meet us here tomorrow around twelve noon and watch what God does to your hood."

The Pasadena police chaplain was right there with the church in the Bloods' hood, being amazed at what was taking place with the church and the Bloods.

Mommu (the mother of the slain child) was still holding MD's hand and looked up into his face and said, "Do you mind if the pastor prayed for you all?"

But MD was moved upon by the Spirit of the Lord and said, "We would like for you to pray for us." Tears were rolling down his face, and all of his homeboys came over to him and Mommu. They knew how bad he must have been feeling, knowing he was the shooter, and they all agreed that they wanted Mommu to pray for them.

Mommu said, "Of course, I will."

The pastor asked the Bloods, "Why have you asked Mommu to pray for you all?"

MD said, "I do not know."

But God gave D-Rock a word of knowledge, and he just blurted out, "There is a special anointing on her to pray for us."

The pastor said, "Amen."

All of the Bloods looked at D-Rock, as if to say, "Where did that come from?"

D-Rock said, "That just came out of me, Blood."

The pastor said, "That was a word of knowledge from the Lord. Now let's make a tighter circle."

The Bloods were in the middle of the whole congregation as Mommu started praying for them.

Narrator

Mommu was asking the Lord to give her the words to pray for the Bloods that would move them toward Him. He answered her prayer by giving her the prayer of Manasseh. She did not know that she was praying the prayer of Manasseh. She just knew that God gave her that prayer for them all.

Mommu's prayer

Lord Almighty, God of our ancestors, God of Abraham, Isaac, and Jacob, God of their righteous descendants, You created the universe and all the splendor that fills it. The sea obeys Your command and never overflows its bounds. The power of Your wonderful, glorious name keeps the ocean depths in their place. When You show Your power, all creation trembles. Your glorious splendor is overwhelming, and Your anger is more than sinners can endure. But the mercy You promise is also greater than we can understand or measure. For You are the Lord Most High. You are patient and show mercy and compassion. You make our punishment easier to bear when we suffer for our sins.

O Lord, in Your great goodness and mercy, You promise forgiveness and salvation to those who repent of their sin against You. You, Lord, are the God of righteous people. Repentance was not necessary for Abraham, Isaac, and Jacob for they did not sin against You. But for sinners like us, You have made repentance possible. We have committed more sins than there are grains of sand on the seashore. There are so many, Lord. There are so many. We have done so much that is wrong that we are not worthy to turn our faces toward heaven. We are crushed beneath the weight of our sins. We are bowed down by its heavy iron chain. We can find no relief for we have made You angry. We have set up idols everywhere. We have done what You hate. But now we bow in deep humility, praying for Your mercy. We have sin. We confess the wicked things we have done. We beg You, Lord. We earnestly pray. Forgive us, forgive us. Do not destroy us because of our sins. Do not stay angry with us forever or store up punishment for us. Do not condemn us to the world of the dead for You, Lord, forgive those who repent. Show us Your mercy and kindness, and save us even though we do not deserve it. Then we will go on praising You as long as we live. All the heavenly powers sing Your praises, and Your glory endures forever. In Jesus's name, amen!

*****

After that prayer, MD asked Mommu, "Why did you keep saying we and us instead of them or they? That prayer sounded like you were also praying for your church too?"

Mommu said, "Son, we all fall short of the glory of God. We do not want y'all to think that you are the only ones that need God. Everyone needs God, and everyone needs prayer no matter who they are."

She could tell that there was something else on MD's mind, so she put her hand gently on the side of MD's face and asked, "What's on your mind, son?"

As tears were coming down his face, he asked Mommu, "How could you be so forgiving?"

She said, "Listen very closely. I am a born-again Christian. God is my father, Jesus Christ is my big brother and savior, and the Holy Spirit is my guide, my teacher, as well as my comforter. The only way I could have all three of them in my life is that I had to be forgiven for the wrongs I have done. The person I was before I gave my life to Christ was a terrible sinner, but God forgave me. Jesus Christ died for me.

"Since they did that for me and they now live in me, it's easy for me to forgive those who wrong me. Listen, let me explain it like this. God did not respond to our sin with revenge or hatred. He responded with love and forgiveness, which in turn, allowed us to respond to His love with love. Yes, it's true. We love Him because He loved us first. So as I respond with Love and forgiveness to those who wrong me, it is my prayer that they will respond with love and also forgive themselves for their past wrongdoings/sins. Hate calls for the response of hate. Love calls for the response of love. So please know that the church loves all of you Bloods and the Crips too. So all you guys have to do is repent and ask God for forgiveness, and He will make you a new person."

MD asked, "I know what asking for forgiveness is, but what do you mean when you say that we must repent?"

Mommu said, "Repentance means to turn from your evil ways. Stop doing the things that does not please God. Be afflicted and mourn and weep. Let your laughter be turned into mourning and joy to heaviness. Humble yourselves in the sight of the Lord, and He will lift you up."

She looked at MD (still not knowing that he was the one that killed her son) and remembered the tears coming down his face when she was holding his hand, and she told him, "Those tears that you were shedding a minute ago was your laughter being turned into mourning. You are halfway home to the law of repentance. God will complete that, which He has already started in you all. The mere fact that you all gave Him this little time to hear Him speak through us, the church, His Son, Jesus Christ, by way of the Holy Spirit, is honored and pleased that you all gave Him even a mustard seed of time. A mustard seed does much more than people can even imagine. We all love you guys, and we hope to see you all here tomorrow as we finish our laps around your hood."

The pastor said, "We must be going now. We thank you gentlemen for your time." Then he told the congregation to make sure that they were there on time the next day. As the congregation was walking away, they were looking back at the Bloods, waving goodbye. The Bloods were just standing there, waving back.

While all of that was taking place in the Bloods' hood, it was also happening in the Crips' hood with their neighborhood church. God was all over both movements.

O. G. Van woke up on Sunday morning around eight and called Jim Jones to make sure that he was up for their escort of the ladies they promised to take to the church. Jim Jones told O. G. Van to come around to his pad, and he would be ready to go pick up Me-Ma and the lady that they stopped from being beaten by her boyfriend.

Once O. G. Van got to Jim Jones's apartment, he knocked on the door, and Jim Jones's mother answered the door. When she saw that it was O. G. Van, she asked, "Now what are you boys doing up so early on a Sunday morning?"

Jim Jones heard his mother questioning his homeboy as he was walking up behind her, so he answered the question for her. He said, "Momma, where do most Black people go this early on Sunday morning?"

She said, "Most of us go to church."

She said it like she knew that was not where they were going. But once those words got out of her mouth, the Holy Spirit hit her with some revelation knowledge that that was exactly where they were going. She turned around with shock in her eyes, and she looked at her son. She grabbed his hands and asked, "Are you going to church, son?"

Jim Jones held his mother's hand gently and said, "O. G. Van and I are merely escorting Me-Ma and her friend to the church and then picking them up after church to walk them back."

She said, "Praise God. He is answering my prayers. Well, I know Me-Ma, and I heard how y'all saved that lady from being beat up. Do you think that they would mind if I walked with y'all?"

Jim Jones was smiling as he looked at his homeboy and asked him, "What do you think?"

O. G. Van said, "How can we deny such a beautiful mother?"

They both laughed and said, "Of course, you can come along, Momma."

As she went to get her coat, Jim Jones looked at O. G. Van and asked, "What is this thing turning into, Cuz?"

O. G. Van said, "I do not know. Let's just get this over with. We should be done by 11:30 a.m. after we escort them back."

So O. G. Van, Jim Jones, and his mother all walked over to Me-Ma's apartment to pick her and the lady up. As Jim Jones knocked on the door of Me-Ma's, he felt a feeling of peace just came over him. One that he never felt before. He turned around to look at O. G. Van, who was looking back at him, shaking his head yes, as if to say that he also felt that feeling of peace.

When the door opened up, you could hear a Gospel music in the background. It was Rance Allen, singing "Something About the Name Jesus."

The lady that they stopped from being beat up answered the door. Her smile was so big and bright that she made everyone else smile. She said, "Come in please." Then she turned to O. G. Van and said, "Thank you for keeping your word to come and escort us to church."

He just shook his head up and down.

Me-Ma came out of her room and was pleased to see Jim Jones's mother with them. They greeted each other jubilantly as they both knew the significance of these two boys escorting them to church. As the mothers finished hugging, they just stood there staring into each other's spirit. Jim Jones's mother said, "Thank you so much for asking my son to simply walk you to church."

Me-Ma said, "Thank you for raising a son that would accept such an invitation."

Then all three of the women turned to Jim Jones and O. G. Van, and Me-Ma said, "What you two are doing by merely walking us to church and picking us up means a lot to us. More importantly, it means a lot to God."

Jim Jones said, "We are honored."

Me-Ma said, "Now before we go out that door, we have to pray." She reached out her hand to O. G. Van, who could not stop himself from reaching back out to hers, and everyone formed a circle as Jim Jones's mother was asked to pray.

She prayed a prayer of thanks to the Lord for allowing her son and his homeboy to walk them to church, and she prayed for the rest of her son's homeboys to be used to enrich the church. They all said, "In Jesus's name, amen!"

Then they all walked out of the apartment. Me-Ma and Jim Jones's mother sandwiched him by grabbing one of his arms each, as O. G. Van was grabbed by the lady that they saved.

As they got to the front of the projects, they noticed a group of Crips out there, as if they were waiting on something or someone. When the group of Crips saw them coming, they all looked at them shaking their heads yes.

As Jim Jones and his group reached them, one of the Crips, Money Mike, said, "For some reason, we all wanted to walk those nice ladies to church with y'all."

Jim Jones's mother said, "Jesus Christ is the reason."

The Crips could not respond to that, so they just split up and put half of them in front of the escorts and half of them in back of the escorts. The walk only took twenty minutes, but when they got to the church, the Crips seemed to be disappointed that the escort had come to an end. All three of the ladies turned around and thanked them for escorting them, and they reminded them to be back there at 11:30 a.m. so they could escort them back to the projects.

Money Mike just blurted out, "Don't worry, we will be here."

The pastor of the church was looking out of his office window and saw the Crips dropping off his church members. He reached out his hand toward the Crips as they were leaving and prayed over them, thanking the Lord for trusting those Crips with His Son's body. The congregation was pulling up in their cars, walking up to the church, and they all saw the escort taking place. They were strengthened in their faith that God was honoring their obedience of walking laps around the projects.

As the Crips were leaving the church, the whole congregation were reaching out their hands toward them as they each said a silent prayer for them. The Crips started waving their hands back at the church members, not knowing that they were being prayed for instead of being waved goodbye too.

Narrator

Right outside of the church grounds, there were demons in the air (atmosphere) awaiting the Crips to walk back to the projects so they could infiltrate any goodness the Crips were feeling. As the church members in the parking lot reached out their hands toward the Crips in prayer, angels of the Lord rushed over to where the Crips were and started fighting those demons off.

As soon as the Lord's angels started beating those demons off from over the Crips, that's when the Crips all turned around and waved back at the church, as if to say we would be all right. Of course, the Crips did not know that there was a spiritual warfare taking place right above their heads.

*****

As the Crips were walking back to the projects, O. G. Van told Jim Jones, "I never felt this way before, Cuz."

The rest of the Crips all agreed too. Big Lou said, "That was the first time that I ever did anything nice."

They all started laughing and said that they could not wait to go back and pick them up.

The chaplain of the Altadena sheriff's station was at the church, and he saw the Crips walking those ladies to church, and he was blessed to see such a sight. So as the church members all went into the services, he got in his car and road up on the Crips as they were about to enter the projects.

As he pulled up on them, they all just stopped and looked at him as he got out of his car for they still see him as a cop and not a friend or someone who cared for them. He got out of his car and said, "I want to thank you gentlemen for humbling yourselves and walking those ladies to church."

They all shook their heads that it was nothing.

The chaplain told them, "God is going to bless you all."

The Crips could not respond to that because they did not know what he was speaking of.

Right then, the gang task force officers drove up on to the Crips, but they did not see their station chaplain in the middle of the Crips. The task force officers jumped out of their cars. It was two car loads of them, pulling up on about seventeen Crips. The officers had their guns drawn as they got out of their cars, telling the Crips to get down on the ground. The Crips were defiant for they knew that they did not do anything to deserve this type of treatment, so none of them got down on the ground.

The chaplain was in the middle of the Crips, and the officers still did not know it. So one of the officers said, "I'm not going to tell you cowards again. If you do not get on the ground, we are going to start arresting each and every one of you."

The Crips still did not respond. They just stood there mean-mugging the officers. So the officer doing all of the talking told the other officers to start cuffing them. The Crips, all at the same time, took a defensive stance, as if to say, "We are not going to let you cops touch us."

That stance made the officers realized that they might have some problems. One of the officers told the Crips, "Let's not make this harder than it has to be."

The chaplain could not take anymore. So he started walking through the Crips, toward the officers. As he came toward them, they still did not know who he was. They all pointed their guns at him as he came forward with his head held down so they could not see his face.

When he got to the front of the Crips and raised his head, the officers lowered their weapons and asked, "What are you doing here? Why didn't you tell us that you were there?"

The chaplain spoke with anger, and he spoke to the officers just like they were talking to the Crips. "Put those guns down, you cowards, and I'm not going tell you again. And if I have to tell you again, I'll be reporting you all to your captain. These gentlemen have done nothing wrong this morning. As a matter of fact, they very well may have done the most generous thing out of all of us this morning. They just came back from walking three ladies to the church. They are also going to pick them up at 11:30 a.m. and walk them back home. So don't tell me that these gentlemen deserve to have guns drawn on them and told to get on the ground and called cowards."

The officers put their guns in their holsters, and then the one doing all of the talking for the officers said, "You need to watch how you talk to us."

The chaplain was seething as he told those officers with fierce anger, "You officers need to watch how you talk to these civilians. You get what you put out."

The officers just got in their cars and left.

9
CHAPTER

All of that time, the Crips were just standing there listening and watching the chaplain defended them. The chaplain had his back to the Crips as he just stood there with tears coming down his face while he watched the officers drove away.

Jim Jones spoke up, "Hey, chaplain, are you all right?"

The chaplain turned around and looked at the Crips, as the tears kept rolling down his face into his beard. When the Crips saw his tears, they all took one step toward him, as if to console him. The chaplain understood that it was their way of saying, "We appreciate you standing up for us," that that one step toward him was their way of symbolically hugging him.

The chaplain said, "I am so sorry for the way those officers treated you all, but please know that in no way do I feel that way toward you. I, as a man of God, love you all and appreciate all of you. May I explain to you all what just happened in the spiritual realm?"

O. G. Van asked, "What do you mean?"

The chaplain said, "What just happened here was an attack from Satan and his demons. They're trying to steal your joy and your peace that you were feeling after walking those ladies to the church."

Jim Jones said, "Just think about it, Cuz, remember when we were walking back from the church a minute ago, and we all were saying how good we felt to have walked those ladies to church? Then right after we said that, here comes the task force officers messing with us."

The chaplain said, "That's exactly what I am talking about. You Crips are right on point."

O. G. Van said, "So what you are saying is those officers were being misused by Satan?"

The chaplain said, "Exactly right, but the all-knowing God placed me right in the middle of you all so that the officers wouldn't see me so much so that they thought that I was one of y'all."

Jim Jones said, "Since God knew those officers were going to be misused by Satan, He sent you to protect us from their mistreatment."

The chaplain was amazed at how fast the Lord was catching on with these Crips. They were picking up revelation knowledge quicker than some seasoned Christians. He told Jim Jones, "You are exactly right. Now please listen very closely because this is very important. Those officers did not know that they were being misused by Satan."

That statement made the Crips think for a minute because he told them to pay close attention, so they knew that he was trying to make a point. So he continued, "When you Crips have fights, shootings, selling drugs, and anything else that is not a law-abiding citizen would do, you too are being misused by Satan."

When the chaplain said that, all of the Crips just put their heads down. He continued, "Right now, you are in a spiritual warfare. Those officers are not your enemies, neither are the Bloods your enemies. They are just vessels that the real enemy is misusing to keep you all from God. Those people at that church that are praying for you and walking laps of reclamation are vessels that God is using to reclaim you all into His loving arms."

Jim Jones asked, "What do you mean reclaim and back into His arms?"

The chaplain said, "Now we are about to have church. When I say reclaim and back into His arms, I am speaking of His original plan that He created us for. But because of Adam's and Eve's disobedience, we all lost our place in God."

O. G. Van said, "Because of one man's disobedience, we all lost our place in God?"

The chaplain said, "Yes."

Money Mike asked, "What kind of a God blames one man's sin on everyone?"

The chaplain answered with tears in his eyes, "The same kind of God that sent His only Son, Jesus Christ, one man, to die and pay for everyone's sins. So if we could all die because of one man's disobedience, how much more then can we all live unto God for man's obedience?"

Big Lou said, "It feels like we are having church right here, right now."

The chaplain said, "That's exactly what happened. We just had church."

Then he told them that he had to get back to the church, so they all walked him to his car, as if they were also escorting him. As he got in his car to leave, he felt more compassion in his heart for those Crips than he had ever felt for anyone. He drove to the church with tears in his eyes.

The Crips all walked to the back of the projects and wondered what they would do until 11:30 a.m. They were not even thinking about smoking weed or drinking beer. As they all looked around their hood and saw all the trash, they just started picking it up like they were some city workers. They realized that this was the first time that they ever cleaned up their own hood. It felt good to be doing that instead of dirtying it up by selling drugs and beating people up and shooting them.

The chaplain made it back to the church in the Crips' hood, and as he walked into the service, the first people he saw were the three ladies that the Crips escorted to the church. As soon as they made eye contact with him, he walked over to where they were sitting and sat in between them. They could tell that he had just went through something.

Jim Jones's mother asked him, "Is everything all right?"

He looked them in their eyes and told them what had just happened with the Crips and himself and the gang task force.

Me-Ma said, "Those Crips and Bloods don't have a chance without God. Then again, no one has a chance without God."

The chaplain just sat there with tears coming down his face for it was his station officers that were out there tripping on the Crips.

While the Crips were waiting around for 11:30 a.m. to come so they could pick up their escorts from church, it dawned on them that they were not drinking beer or smoking weed. What they were really tripping on was the fact that they did not have the desire to do so.

Narrator

The Crips did not know that those same angels that fought off those demons that were assigned to them were still hovering over them, protecting them from Satan's demons.

*****

As 11:30 a.m. was approaching, the Crips could not help but feel the anticipation of going to pick up their escorts. The mere fact that they were doing something noble really touched them in their spirit man. Even though they did not fully understand it, it felt good, and it was the first time that they ever did something good consciously. God was softening their hearts so that they will be ready to receive Him when He would be presented to them in the very near future.

Well, as the Crips arrived back at the church to pick up their escorts, the church members were all going out from the service to go home and have some lunch and put on some walking shoes and change their clothes so they could meet back at the church to start their fifth lap around the projects.

The pastor walked up to the Crips and thanked them for their escorting services. He also told them that the chaplain of the sheriff's station told him what went down with the gang task force officers, and he apologized for that.

Jim Jones said, "It happens every time we see those officers. It just so happened that God has His own chaplain in the middle of us, showing them what those officers are capable of."

The pastor said, "The Lord is protecting you all. That is His way of showing you that He appreciates you taking the time to escort His children to and from church."

O. G. Van said, "That is the way that we see it too."

As the pastor was shaking their hands, the three ladies that they were escorting walked up. The Crips immediately surrounded them in a protective shield. They were really proud to be escorting those three ladies.

As they were walking back to the projects, the lady that the Crips stopped from being beat up walked up to O. G. Van and put her arm through his. Jim Jones's mother put her arm through his and Me-Ma put her arm through two of the other Crips' arms. They just all silently walked back to their hood.

When they got to the projects, the Crips who did not have their arms tied up walked to the front of the gates and made a walkway for them to walk through. The escorted ladies walked to their respective apartments with the Crips, who were in arm in arm with them. Me-Ma told the lady that was with O. G. Van to invite him over for dinner that evening. She was more than please to do so for she really enjoyed being around him. So she asked him if he would like to come over for dinner that night.

O. G. Van was not ready for that, but he was glad that she asked for he really enjoyed being around her too. But it was really hard on him being at that apartment where a bullet that he fired hit and killed a little girl. And now they were inviting him to come over and have dinner there. They could tell that he was nervous by the way he was acting and looking at his homeboy, Jim Jones.

So Me-Ma asked Jim Jones, "Will you come too?"

Everyone could see the relief that came over O. G. Van for whatever Jim Jones's answer would be the answer for both of them.

Jim Jones could not turn them down, so he said, "We will both be there."

Me-Ma said, "Good, you two be here at 6:00 p.m."

O. G. Van and Jim Jones left that apartment feeling really loved. As they were walking away, they looked back at the apartment where they just came from, and the lady that O. G. Van escorted to church and stopped from being beat up by her boyfriend was in the window watching him. When he made eye contact with her, she waved bye to him. O. G. Van's heart just melted.

He told Jim Jones, "I never felt these feelings before."

"What type of feelings are you feeling?" Jim Jones asked.

O. G. Van answered, "I feel all soft." That was the only way that he could describe it.

Meanwhile, down in the Bloods' hood, they were kicking back in the projects, talking about what the church in their hood was doing. They couldn't deny the light that was hovering over their projects or the fact that right outside of the projects, that same light did not exist.

There was about sixty Bloods just sitting there thinking about all that was taking place in their hood. MD spoke up, "Have y'all noticed that there have not been any Crips riding around looking for us or how we ourselves have not been riding around looking for any of them?"

One of the Bloods said, "I have not even been thinking about the Crips." They all agreed that they have not either.

As they were talking, the light over their hood seemed to get a little brighter than it already was. So much so that the Bloods stopped talking and looked up into the sky, then they heard the choir singing "He Is Here" right outside of their projects. All of the Bloods walked to the front of the projects and saw the whole church walking laps around their hood. The last two people in the line of the procession of about two hundred people, all walking in twos, just like God sent the disciples out—two by two—were the Pasadena police chaplain and Mommu (the mother of the slain child that the Bloods mistakenly killed). When she made eye contact with MD (the actual shooter of her child which she did not know), she stopped and reached out to him.

MD knew that she was the mother of the child that he accidentally shot, and so did his homeboys know. In a daze, MD walked over to her and grabbed her hand. He tried to say something (he was about to confess that it was him that shot her son), but she put her finger to his lips and turned back to the line, continuing her march with MD by her side.

The police chaplain beckoned the rest of the Bloods to fall in line. As if in a trance, they fell in line in twos, following the congregation. The people in the front of the line did not even realize that the Bloods had gotten in line. The only two that knew were Mommu and the police chaplain.

The choir was singing and the deacons were reading Joshua 6 and the pastor was praying in tongues. Everyone else was walking in silence. This was the seventh day, so they were to walk seven full laps. The Bloods did not question anything. They just obediently walked with the congregation. When Mommu noticed all of the Bloods behind her in line, walking laps along with the church, she was spiritually moved with the compassion of God.

The church was walking around the projects to take back their youths and their neighborhood from Satan's bondage, and here it was on the final day of laps, all of the Bloods with their red rags and red clothing (their gang colors) were in the line of lap walkers. Only the power of God could be so movable.

Mommu could feel God all over her. She actually felt blessed that her son was in heaven with God and Jesus Christ. And because she accepted the spiritual fact that her son was with God, God had blessed her with many more sons in the Bloods gang. She knew that Satan meant for the death of her son to be evil and cause more death and pain, but God meant it unto good and for it to be taken as life so that many could live in Christ. She knew and believed that just as God sent His Son, Jesus Christ, to pay and die for our sins so that we could live in Him and not die and go to hell and just as Jesus Christ was raised from the dead, defeating death, so it was with her son's passing. Now because of the death and resurrection of Jesus Christ, God has many more children/sons to call His own and Jesus Christ has many more brothers and sisters, so it was with Mommu. She had many more children and her son in heaven had many more brothers and sisters.

As they continued their laps around the projects, it just kept getting brighter and brighter over their hood, as if some*one* (the Father, the Son, and the Holy Ghost—these three are One; thus, we have some*one*) was turning a light on higher and higher.

The church knew that it was God honoring their mission to take back what the enemy stole. The Bloods were simply amazed at what peace they were feeling and at the miracle of light over their hood. As they came to the end of their last lap, Mommu, who was holding the hand of her child's killer (unbeknownst to her), looked up into the bright light over the Bloods' hood. And she was the first to see cherubim (angels) all standing in midair in one full circle, all the way around the projects, the Bloods' hood, with the armor of God on. They had shields and double-edged swords in their hands, and there was no demon in sight. She pointed up to the heavens, and the whole congregation looked up, and when they saw the angels posted up in a protective stance, they all started praising God in tongues and shouts of hallelujahs.

The Bloods all thought that they were tripping off on the light over their hood. The church surrounded the Bloods gang, reaching their hands toward them and praying in tongues. As they were doing that, the Bloods all just stood there, as if in full submission to the Spirit of the Lord.

Mommu was still holding MD's hand as she was looking up at the angels with tears coming down her face. All that the Bloods could see was the light. They could not see that angels yet.

The pastor walked up to the Bloods, as the church was still praying in tongues, with hands stretched out toward them. The Pasadena police chaplain was standing with the pastor as the pastor told the Bloods, "You gentlemen and this neighborhood have been reclaimed from the spirit of Satan and his demons. That bright light you see over your hood is the Lord Himself. He is showing you all a visible miracle so that you would believe what He is telling you through us, His body [the Church]. All that you've done before now—the shootings, beatings, robberies, stabbings, burglaries, and even murder—you've done those things under the spirit of Satan and his demons. What God is really saying to you all is that He does not blame you neither do we, the church. We do not hold anything against you about your past crimes and sins. For we know that you do not understand the spiritual aspects/facts of life and death. But after today, if you do not choose life, God will hold you accountable because of what is being explained to you right now by Him through us, His body, the church.

"This set up here, right now, is the equivalent of God calling heaven and earth as witnesses against you that He has set before you—life and death, blessings and cursing. Therefore, choose life that both you and your seed shall live.

"God will not force His will on you. The choice is yours to either serve Him or the devil. He is now asking you all through us, His body, to accept His Son, Jesus Christ, as Lord of your lives. If any of you Bloods wish to represent the *blood* of Jesus Christ, which cleanses, instead of the blood of Satan, which kills, just step forward, and I will lead in to a prayer that will give you a brand-new life in Jesus Christ. It will be as if your past life never existed. That's how new you will be."

Mommu looked up into MD's eyes (her child's killer) and led him to the pastor. Once MD got in front of the pastor, he just broke down crying and fell to his knees. All the rest of the Bloods stepped forward and also fell to their knees. The whole congregation was still praying in tongues with their hands stretched toward them.

The pastor raised his hands and looked up into heaven and said, "Thank You, Father."

The church fell silent as the pastor asked the Bloods to repeat after him, as he led them in a prayer that would give their lives to Jesus Christ. After they all repeated the sinner's prayer of repentance and acceptance of Jesus Christ as Lord of their lives, the church rejoiced, and they all started hugging the Bloods, welcoming them into the family of God.

Now the Bloods were Christians, and after they got done hugging the congregation, MD looked up into the light over their hood, and he saw the angels in God's armor standing in a protective stance, all the way around their projects. He told his homeboys, who were now his brothers in Christ, to look up and see the angels.

The pastor knew that they could now see the angels, so he explained to them that those angels were there to keep Satan and his demons out of the way of this movement.

MD said, "What an awesome God we now serve."

All of the rest of the Bloods were saying things like, "No one can tell me that God does not exist" and "We had it wrong all of this time."

Meanwhile, back in the Crips' hood, Jim Jones and O. G. Van were chilling in the projects with all of their homeboys. They were tripping on the fact that they were not drinking beer and smoking weed and selling drugs. The kids were out playing like this was a different neighborhood. Plus, there was still that light over their hood that none of them could explain. Even at night, the moon would seem to line up right over their projects so that it would be brighter right over their hood than it was anywhere else.

Jim Jones and O. G. Van told their homeboys that they were going to go have that dinner that they were invited to have.

Big Lou asked O. G. Van, "Are you cool with going back over to that apartment?" They all knew that it was his bullet that killed that little girl that lived there.

O. G. Van said, "I do not know how I feel about it, Cuz, but I do feel myself being pulled over there, and I do not even know what that means."

Jim Jones said, "Let's go, Cuz."

Their homeboys said that they would stay posted up in the hood.

When O. G. Van and Jim Jones got to Me-Ma's apartment, the door swung open before they had a chance to knock. It was the little boy, Me-Ma's son. He was all smiles because he really liked Jim Jones and O. G. Van ever since he met them when he was looking for his sister's killer (not knowing that O. G. Van was the killer). Smooth asked them to come in and have seat. They went in and had a seat, as they smelled some good food being cooked in the kitchen.

Jim Jones said, "That sure smells good."

Smooth said, "Yeah, my momma can cook."

O. G. Van asked, "What is she cooking?"

Smooth answered, "Steaks and rice, corn, biscuits, and some salad."

O. G. Van and Jim Jones looked at each other, shaking their heads yes.

Me-Ma came out of the kitchen with two glasses of some iced orange juice and gave them to O. G. Van and Jim Jones. The lady that invited O. G. Van to dinner was setting the table.

Me-Ma said, "Ayo, come say hi to your guest, girl."

Jim Jones said, "Thank you, Me-Ma, for this invitation."

O. G. Van said, "I cannot remember the last time that I smelled something so good that it made my stomach growl like it is right now."

Ayo came over and said, "I'm glad you came, and I am also happy to hear that you like what you smell."

Me-Ma said, "Yeah, because she is the one that did the cooking, and that girl can burn."

Jim Jones said, "Your son said that you can really cook too, and we thought you did the cooking."

Me-Ma said, "What else would a son say about his momma's cooking? He thought that I was cooking, but I was just helping Ayo out."

Ayo said, "That's enough talking now. Let's get in the dining room and eat." She looked at O. G. Van and smiled at him, and he was blushing, all nervous.

Jim Jones said, "Cuz, I have never seen you so scared." And they all started laughing.

When they got to the dinner table, Jim Jones asked, "Where do we sit, Me-Ma?"

Me-Ma said, "Jim Jones, you sit next to me. O. G. Van, you sit at the head of the table, like the man of the house. Smooth, you know where you sit, and Ayo, I know you know where you sit at."

There was only one seat left, and it was right next to O. G. Van, so Ayo sat next to him. Everyone saw O. G. Van's chest pumped with pride.

After everyone was seated, Me-Ma asked Smooth to say grace. He said a short prayer of thanks for the food, but before he ended the prayer, he asked God to let Jim Jones and O. G. Van be his big brothers.

Jim Jones and O. G. Van were truly touched by his request to the Lord, and Jim Jones told him, "We will be your big brothers if you really want us to be."

Smooth just looked up into heaven and said, "Thank You, Father."

10
CHAPTER

The food was so good that O. G. Van and Jim Jones could not even speak.

Me-Ma said, "You boys sure know how to eat. I see y'all did not come here to do any talking." Everyone laughed. Then the phone started ringing, so Me-Ma excused herself and went to answer it. It was the Altadena sheriff chaplain, and he told her that he got a phone call from the Pasadena police chaplain and was told that the church in the Bloods' hood had completed their laps and that right at the end of their seventh lap, the Bloods all committed their lives to the Lord. He went on to tell her how awesome God was and how the Bloods even walked a few of the last laps with the church. Me-Ma just sat down as the chaplain was explaining it all to her. Tears were coming down her pretty face as she was listening to that beautiful testimony.

Her son, Smooth, saw his mother crying, so he walked over to where she was and put his hand on her shoulder, and she grabbed his hand and held it. The chaplain said that he would be in touch with her, and she said, "Okay," and hung up the phone. She walked back to the dinner table where everyone was at.

Jim Jones asked, "Is everything all right, Me-Ma?"

She said, "Yes, son. Let's finish eating, and then I will share the lovely testimony that I just heard over the phone."

Ayo asked O. G. Van and Jim Jones if they wanted more, and they declined, wanting to hear that testimony from Me-Ma. Everyone was finished, and Ayo and Smooth cleared the table.

Me-Ma told everyone to come into the living room so they could talk. She waited for Ayo and Smooth to come out of the kitchen before she speaks. Ayo and Smooth came out of the kitchen, and Ayo went and sat right next to O. G. Van. He felt so blessed to have her sitting next to him.

Me-Ma said, "I just got off from the phone with the Altadena sheriff chaplain. He told me the most blessed news that I've heard in a long time." Then she looked at Jim Jones and O. G. Van, tears ran down here pretty face, and said, "The Bloods have all given their lives to the Lord, Jesus Christ."

Jim Jones asked, "What did you just say?"

So Me-Ma repeated herself to them, "The Bloods have all given their lives to the Lord, Jesus Christ. God has honored that church's obedience of reclaiming those youths and their hood from the enemy by walking those laps around their hood."

Jim Jones asked, "You mean the church in their hood was doing the same thing that the church in our hood is doing?"

Me-Ma said, "Yes, son, they started doing it a few days before us. They finished their laps today, and the power of God moved upon the Bloods to become His children."

O. G. Van said, "So what you are telling us is that the Bloods are not gangbanging anymore."

Me-Ma said, "They probably are still gangbanging, but now they are banging for the Lord, Jesus Christ, not Satan."

Jim Jones said, "I'll have to see that to believe that."

Me-Ma responded, "There is a brother in the Bible that said the same thing, and Jesus Christ showed him, just like He is going to show you."

O. G. Van asked, "What was the brother's name in the Bible?"

Me-Ma said, "They called him doubting Tomas." Then she asked Jim Jones, "Can you go get all of your homeboys?"

He said that they were right outside waiting on him and O. G. Van.

Me-Ma said, "Make sure y'all don't make any plans to move on the Bloods."

Jim Jones said, "We are not tripping on them right now. Ever since this light has been hanging over our hood and that sheriff chaplain came to our defense after we walked y'all to church, we have not even thought about them Bloods."

Me-Ma asked Jim Jones, "Please go get all of your homeboys so I can speak to them?"

He said that of course, he would.

Me-Ma got up out of her seat and went to open the front door for Jim Jones to go get them.

He asked, "You mean right now?"

She said, "Yes."

So as he was getting up to leave, O. G. Van rose up to go with him, but Me-Ma asked him to please wait there with her and Ayo. Jim Jones told him to just chill, and he would be back with the homies.

As Jim Jones was walking to the back of the projects, his mind was reeling with the events that had taken place since those two shootings.

As he approached his homeboys, they were simply kicking back, talking about the chaplain sticking up for them against the gang task force. When they saw Jim Jones, they all stood up, and one of them asked, "Where is O. G. Van at, Cuz?"

They all felt like they had to look out for O. G. Van because they all knew how bad he felt about killing that little girl. Plus, he was having dinner with the little girl's mother and brother.

Jim Jones said, "He is at Me-Ma's place, and she wants all of us to come over there so she can talk to us."

Big Lou asked, "What does she want with all of us, Cuz?"

Jim Jones said, "While we were there eating dinner, she got a phone call from the Altadena sheriff chaplain, and he told her that he got a phone call from the Pasadena police chaplain, who told him that the Bloods have all given their lives to Jesus Christ today."

The Crips all started talking at the same time. "They did what?"

"Are you serious?"

"I don't believe it."

Jim Jones said, "Let's go hear what she has to say."

As they were walking over to her apartment, one of the Crips said, "I ain't about to become no Bible thumper. I'm telling y'all now." No one said anything in response.

They were all thinking about what Jim Jones had said about the Bloods becoming Christians.

While Jim Jones went to get his homeboys, O. G. Van asked Me-Ma, "What does it mean that the Bloods gave their lives to Jesus Christ?"

She answered, "It means that all of their crimes and sins have been paid for, forgiven, and wiped out, as if they never did them. Jesus Christ died and paid for them all. Since the Bloods believe it and have confess with their mouths that Jesus Christ is the Lord of their lives, they are now Christians. Jesus Christ is their big brother."

O. G. Van asked, "Does that mean that the Bloods will not be coming after us Crips anymore to stab, shoot, and fight?"

She said, "My poor boy, listen to what I am about to say to you very carefully."

Just as she was about to speak, her doorbell rang. Ayo went to answer it, and it was Jim Jones and his homeboys. They were about thirty of them. Me-Ma went to the door and saw that it was too many of them to come into her apartment, so she told them all to wait one second. Me-Ma told O. G. Van to get one of her chairs out of the kitchen and bring it out to the front porch. O. G. Van brought the chair out to the porch and held the back of it for Me-Ma to sit down on it. Then he heard Ayo dragging a chair for herself, and he turned around and got it for her. He also held the back of her chair so that she could sit down.

Me-Ma told the Crips to gather around so she could talk to them for a minute. Before she started speaking, more Crips started showing up. The neighbors started realizing the crowd at Me-Ma's apartment. Some of them got nervous when they saw all of those Crips, so they called the sheriffs to come quickly because the Crips were about to do something at the lady's apartment where that kid was killed the other week.

That's all the gang task force needed to hear for they were waiting to show their station chaplain that the Crips were evil. The chaplain heard the call over his office scanner, and when he came out of his office, he saw the gang task force putting on their SWAT armor, as if they were going to a full-scale riot.

Narrator

There was a full-scale riot going on, but it was not the Crips and Bloods fighting each other. It was God's angels fighting Satan's demons off right outside of the projects in the atmosphere. Satan knew that he had already lost the Pasadena Denver Lane Blood Gang, so he was fighting hard not to lose the Altadena Block Crips.

*****

The chaplain asked the task force sergeant what was happening, the sergeant said, "The Crips are about a hundred deep in the projects. Something is about to jump off."

"How do you know this?" the chaplain asked.

"We got a phone call from a scared tenant in the projects."

The chaplain went into his office and called the Pasadena police chaplain and asked him if the Bloods were preparing to have a riot with the Crips.

The Pasadena police chaplain said, "No, as matter of fact, I am on my way to the church because there was a surprise blessing for the Bloods, and all of them are meeting us at the church."

The Altadena sheriff chaplain said, "A call just came over the scanner here that the Crips were about a hundred deep in the projects and a riot or something is about to jump off. The task force got in full riot gear and are responding."

The Pasadena police chaplain assured him that it was not the Bloods that the Crips were tripping on and then told him that he would meet him at the Altadena block projects in about fifteen minutes.

*****

Me-Ma said, "First of all, I want you all to know that God loves you and so do I."

One of the Crips hollered from the back, "We love you too, Me-Ma."

She continued, "Now we are going to address that love you say that you have for me. Don't get me wrong. Now I really do appreciate you saying that you love me. But I want you all to know that the only way you can sincerely love me or anyone else, for that matter, is to sincerely love God. If you do not love God, who has sent His only begotten Son to die and pay for your sins, how can you love me, who has done nothing for you? I'm not saying that you do not believe or really think that you love me. But I do not think that you all know what love really is."

As soon as she said that, tears started rolling down her pretty face. She continued, "Who out of you all can tell me what love really is?" No one answered her. So she asked the one Crip that said that they love her to step forward. She asked him, "What is your name, son?"

He said, "Keenan."

She asked him, "What is your love for me?"

He said, "I just respect and care for you."

She said, "That's sweet, baby, but would you die for me? Would you be tortured for me? Be whipped on for me? Spit on for me? Would you do all of that for me even if you never met me?"

Keenan said, "I do not know anyone that would go through all of that for someone that they know, let alone for someone that they do not know."

She said, "I'm going to introduce you to some*one* who has already done all of that and more for all of us. Let me ask you something. Listen very carefully, say you ran up to me all scared because you saw a bullet with your name on it, and it was coming right at you, and even I saw it as you were talking to me, and you told me that you knew you were about to die and that you knew you deserved to die for all the wrongdoings that you've done to people. So you tell me that you wish you had one more chance to apologize to those you've wronged and let your mother know that you love her very much, and you even said that you wanted to ask God to forgive you and let Him know that you do believe that His Son is the Savior and that you accept Him as Lord of your life. Now you know at least that you will be going to heaven when that bullet hits and kills you.

"Well, just as that bullet hits and kills you, I jumped in front of you, and the bullet hit and killed me. Would you then go do all of those things that you said you wish you had the chance to do? Apologize to those you've wronged, tell your mother that you love her, and ask God to forgive you, and accept His Son and Lord so you could go to heaven? Would any of you Crips do what he said he wished he had a chance to do after I took that bullet for him and died? Would you? How many of you can give me your word and say that you would do all of those things that he said he wanted to have a one more chance to do if I took that bullet meant for you and I died instead of you?"

They all raised their hands. She asked, "Are all of you men of your words?"

They all said, "Of course, we are."

She said, "Would you do it if that person who took that bullet and died for you was some*one* that you did not even know?"

They said, "Of course, we would."

She said, "Now remember that you are men of your words."

They said again, "We are men of our words."

Me-Ma said, "I'm about to find out right now."

Keenan said, "There is no bullet coming at us right now, and bullets don't have names on them."

Me-Ma said, "The bullet I'm talking about is the sin in your lives, and it is already killing you. The person I'm talking about that has jumped in front of that bullet is Jesus Christ. He jumped in front of that bullet for you before you were even born into that sin. He took your punishment and paid for your sins. Now you all told me that you were men of your words. We are about to find out who is and who is not. You all said that you would apologize to those you wronged, tell your mothers that you love them, and ask God to forgive you and accept His Son as Lord of your lives so you could all go to heaven. Well, it was all done for you. Jesus Christ died and paid for your sins."

Right after she said that, a few of the Crips were about to come forward and ask her what they had to do to accept Jesus Christ as Lord of their lives, but the task force pulled up into the projects, four cars deep, they jumped out of their cars with guns drawn, telling the Crips not to move.

None of the Crips would even look at the task force officers. They stayed focus on Me-Ma.

So Me-Ma asked the officers, "What is the problem?"

They told her, "We received a phone a call that the Crips were grouping up and something was about to go down with them."

Me-Ma said, "I called all of these young men over here to tell them about the Lord Jesus. Ain't nothing wrong with that, is it?"

The officers did not want to hear that, so they turned on the Crips and told them to start breaking it up and to move along.

Money Mike said, "Man, we ain't going nowhere. We ain't doing anything wrong. Plus, this is where we live."

The officer said, "I else, the Altadena sheriff chaplain."

They both jumped out of their cars and asked the officers what was going on.

The gang task officers did not like their chaplains because they felt that they were sympathizers for the Crips and the Bloods, so the officers just looked at them with disgust in their eyes.

Jim Jones walked up to the Altadena sheriff chaplain and said, "We were all over here chilling with Me-Ma, hearing about the Bloods becoming Christians, when these task force officers rolled up on us and tripping, telling us to break it up and move on."

The chaplain said, "You guys do not have to go nowhere."

The officers looked at the chaplains, and the task force sergeant said, "We are getting tired of you chaplains interfering with us doing our job."

The officers got in their cars and left.

The chaplain told the Chips once again that he was sorry for his station officers' actions, but they got a phone call that something was about to happen, like some type of riot was about to take place.

Jim Jones said, "Who are we going to have a riot with? I thought the Bloods gave their lives to the Lord."

Both chaplains said, "They have."

O. G. Van said, "That is still hard to believe."

The Pasadena chaplain said, "It may be hard to believe, but it's true."

11
CHAPTER

The Pasadena police chaplain asked, "Can I bring one or two of the Bloods to meet with one or two of you Crips? Just so that they can tell you themselves that it's true."

Jim Jones said, "O. G. Van and myself will meet them."

While they were talking, one of Me-Ma's neighbors, an elderly lady named Hattie-Mae, walked up and said, "Me-Ma, may I say something to them?"

Me-Ma said, "Go ahead, Sister Hattie-Mae."

She said, "I was the one that called the sheriff officers because I was afraid when I saw all of you Crips coming over to Me-Ma's apartment. Especially, since her daughter was killed." She then looked at the Crips and asked, "Please forgive me for misjudging you all?"

O. G. Van walked up to Sister Hattie-Mae and said, "Of course, we forgive you, and now we would like to ask you and Me-Ma to please forgive us for all of the wrongdoings that we have done in this neighborhood?"

Sister Hattie-Mae reached her hand up to his face and gently touched him there and said, "Of course, we forgive you all."

At the touch of Sister Hattie-Mae's hand to the side of his face, O. G. Van never felt such a calming spirit came over him as he did at that moment. By this time, all of the neighbors had come out of their apartments because they could feel the peace of the gathering. So there was about a 150 people in front of Me-Ma's apartment. Most of them were church members, and they started inviting the Crips to march with them and to come to the church with them.

Well, the church in the Crips' hood had two more days of laps to go. The Crips did not show up for one of them, but they all showed up for the last day of laps. Before the last laps were marched around the Crips' projects, the chaplains from both police and sheriff situations got Jim Jones and O. G. Van together with two of the Bloods. It was MD and D-Rock.

They met up at Bob's Big Boy restaurant in downtown Pasadena, right across the street from Pasadena City College. Although the Bloods (MD and D-Rock) were born-again Christians, they were still wearing their red gang colors in clothing. Jim Jones and O. G. Van noticed their red clothing before they even realized the individuals wearing those colors.

Narrator

That's how Satan works. He will have people tripping off on worldly things instead of godly things. There were times when the Crips and the Bloods would see someone wearing blue or red clothing and just start beating on that person just for wearing those colors, regardless if they were gangbangers or not.

*****

The Altadena sheriff chaplain was the escort for Jim Jones and O. G. Van (the Crips) while the Pasadena police chaplain was the escort for MD and D-Rock (the Bloods).

When the two groups saw each other, the chaplains greeted each other and then they introduced the Crips and the Bloods to each chaplain. Then they turned their attention to the four that were there to meet each other.

The Bloods were truly born-again Christians, so they felt at ease about the meeting. The two Crips were not yet born again, but their hearts had been softened by all of the past events in their hood by the church. The Bloods actually got out of their seats and extend their hands to the Crips. They shook hands and then looked at the chaplains who told them to have a seat.

85

A waiter came to their table and set menus before them. They all ordered first, then when the waiter took their orders and left the table, the Altadena sheriff chaplain spoke first, "MD, will you please tell these two Crips what happened with you and your homeboys?"

MD said, "I do not know how to explain it."

D-Rock said, "Neither do I."

The Pasadena police chaplain said, "Just speak, and God will give you the words."

So MD said, "Look, man, our whole hood, the Pasadena Denver Lane Blood Gang, has given our lives over to the Lord, Jesus Christ. His Spirit just came over us right there in our hood. The church in our hood did some type of walk around our hood for seven days."

Jim Jones interrupted him and asked, "Did your hood get a little brighter with each lap, as if someone turned on a light in a room and that room was your hood, but right outside of your hood, that same light did not exist?"

MD said, "Exactly, how did you know that?"

Jim Jones said, "The same thing has been happening in our hood."

The Altadena sheriff chaplain said that the church in the Crips' hood had one more day of laps to go.

MD continued, "Well, man, all I can tell you is that on the last day of laps, we were all moved upon by the Spirit of the Lord, and we all gave our lives to Him. Every last one of us. Not one of us was untouched."

D-Rock spoke up, "I never felt anything like it."

O. G. Van said, "I've been feeling something moving inside of me too, but I cannot explain it."

MD said, "That's the Spirit of the Lord preparing your heart to receive His Son, Jesus Christ, as your Savior."

All of sudden, Jim Jones looked up at MD and said, "I thought you did not know how to explain it?"

MD said, "That ain't me speaking. It's the Spirit of the Lord. Like the chaplain said, if I just open my mouth, the Lord would speak for me."

They all laughed.

MD said, "It's funny, but that's what really happened. God just spoke through me to you." Tears just began to roll down MD's face because he was so touched that God would actually speak through him.

Narrator

Here they were having lunch and testifying of what God was doing in their lives. MD, the Blood who accidentally shot and killed the little boy in his hood as he was trying to shoot the Crips, and O. G. Van, the Crip who accidentally shot and killed the little girl in his hood as he was trying to shoot the Bloods.

Satan and his demons were so mad that they were actually trying to get into the restaurant and do some damage. But God had His angels posted up around the restaurant, and the demons saw them and knew they had no chance. All of that was taking place in the atmosphere, right over the restaurant.

*****

The chaplain told MD that what he just said was scriptural.

MD said, "I can feel Him speaking through me because the person I used to be would not have known to say any of those things that were just said through me."

D-Rock looked at MD and said, "That's pretty deep, homie."

Jim Jones said, "So it is true, huh? Y'all are Christians now?"

MD said, "Yeah, we are all Christians now."

So the food came, and the chaplain said grace over the food, and they all ate. After the meal, the Pasadena police chaplain said that they had a surprise for the Bloods at the church and all of the Bloods would be there waiting on them. The Altadena sheriff chaplain asked if they could stop by on their way back to Altadena. That question was very much answered with favor.

Jim Jones and O. G. Van wanted to see this surprise themselves, so they agreed to stop by with the Altadena sheriff chaplain.

The pastor in the Bloods' hood was just opening the doors to the church when he heard a bunch of noise behind him. When he turned around and saw all of the Bloods pulling up in cars and walking up into the parking lot, he was blessed by that sight.

Now the Bloods had not even had a chance to attend a church service yet, but here they all were, ready to hear what God had in store for them. They all started walking into the church, some of them for the first time ever. Then the Pasadena police chaplain and the Altadena sheriff chaplain pulled up with MD, D-Rock, Jim Jones, and O. G. Van.

It was a sight to see all of those Bloods walking into the church all dressed in their red gang colors. The Bloods all stopped when they saw their homeboys pulling up with the chaplains, but they were caught off guard when they saw Jim Jones and O. G. Van with them dressed in blue (their gang colors).

MD and D-Rock saw the puzzling look on their homeboys' faces and motioned for them to keep on going into the church. As they all piled in, the pastor of the church motioned for everyone to have a seat.

The Pasadena police chaplain and the Altadena sheriff chaplain walked Jim Jones and O. G. Van down to the front of the church and sat them down in front. The Bloods were nodding their heads at Jim Jones and O. G. Van, as if to say, "It's all good." Some of them knew them, and some did not.

O. G. Van asked Jim Jones, "Are you cool, Cuz?"

Jim Jones said, "I'm cool, but I have never been around so many Bloods before."

O. G. Van responded, "Yeah, me neither."

The chaplains walked up to the podium and told the pastor what was up with Jim Jones and O. G. Van being there.

The pastor felt the hand of God all over that. He asked everyone to stand for prayer. As they all stood, the pastor thanked the two Crips for stopping by, and to the Crips' surprise, all of the Bloods started clapping their hands. Even the angels on guard in the atmosphere outside of the church were clapping for that.

As the pastor prayed a prayer of thanks, a group of four men came into the church wearing business suits. They were actual church members there to surprise the Bloods with a special blessing from the Lord.

After the pastor prayed, he noticed the four gentlemen there that were to bless the Bloods. He motioned for them to come forward. As they were coming forward, the pastor told the Bloods, "These four gentlemen are members of our church. Their names are Terry Moses, the creator of the Bounty Hunters Bloods Gang in Watts. He is now serving the Lord after serving time in prison. While he was in prison, he wrote a few books about gangbanging and the pain it causes people. Also, we are honored to have with him one of his close friends and coauthor of one his books, Donovan Simmons from Skyline Piru Bloods Gang in San Diego. He was in prison with Brother T. Moses, and they corroborated on writing a book to touch the lives of those that they have misled.

"Also, here is Brother Quin Epps and Brother Derrick Dobynes, a couple of ex-Bloods from the Sacramento area, now living down here as successful business men and serving the Lord right here out of our church. They too were touched by the Lord while doing time in prison. They learned some trades while in prison and now have their own companies. Bro Quin owns a big-time woodshop, and Bro Derrick owns a big-time welding company. God has blessed all four of these gentlemen with success in everything that they touch. Now they wish to bless you all in a special way."

They all came up behind the pastor, and he gave the mic to Bro T. Moses first, the oldest of the four.

T. Moses said, "First of all, I want to apologize to you all for ever starting a Bloods gang. I am truly sorry and ask that you all forgive me. There will be copies of my books passed out at the end of this service of blessing. One of the books is called *Married to the Streets for Better for Worse*. I'm so bless to see a church full of Bloods. I cannot even explain the feelings I feel right now. It is blowing my mind seeing you all here as Christians. I have something to offer you all, but I want my brothers to give you their short testimonies before we make the offer that God has sent us here to bless y'all with."

As tears were coming down T. Moses's face, he passed the mic to his coauthor, Donovan Simmons. He took the mic and said, "God bless you, brothers."

All of the Bloods said, "God bless you too."

He said, "I receive that. I want to thank you all for showing up. We did not know how many of y'all would come, but we are blessed to see a full house. My gang name was Frank Nitty, and I really thought that banging was all there was. I've seen people killed over colors and words, and I'm sure you all have seen it too. Some of you even put in work on that same tip. Well, I do not need to go into all of that with you all for it is obvious that you all have seen the light. Literally, right over your hood, with each lap we have walked around it. I'm also here to make y'all an offer, but before I do, I'll let these other two brothers speak to y'all."

He handed the mic to Brother Derrick Dobynes who said, "I was a Blood gang member out of Sacramento, and now I'm serving the Lord Almighty. I'm also blessed to see you all out here claiming God as your Father. The pastor pretty much gave y'all my testimony. I went to prison, and the Spirit of the Lord came over me, and I gave Him my life. God blessed me with a welding trade while I was in prison, and I too have an offer for you all, but I'll let my Brother Quin speak before I make my offer."

He handed the mic to Brother Quin. Brother Quin grabbed the mic and said, "What a blessing to see all of you brothers in this church. I also see that you all still have your gang colors on. With that aisle in the middle of y'all, it almost looks like the Red Sea that the Lord parted through Moses."

They all laughed. He continued, "That's okay to be still wearing your colors, just make sure that you are wearing them for a different reason, like for the blood of the Lamb."

T. Moses said, "It ain't about putting new clothes and colors on the man, but it is about putting a new man in those clothes and colors."

Everyone hollered, "Amen!"

Brother Quin went on to say, "Look, we are here as ex-gang members of some Blood gangs, and we are born-again Christians that God has blessed with, and we were all moved upon to make an offer to you all. While I was in prison, I got a trade in woodshop, and God has blessed me with a successful business, and He wants to bless you all, just as He has blessed each and every one of us."

With that being said, the other three walked up beside Bro Quin, and they all gave him the okay sign to continue with their offers. But Bro Quin, being the humble person that he was, gave the mic back to Brother T. Moses, the oldest of the four.

Brother T. Moses took the mic, and as he began to speak, the other three brothers opened up some briefcases that they had and took out a bunch of applications for some trade tech schools. Brother T. Moses said, "We have been moved upon by the Spirit of the Lord to finance you all with a chance to go to any trade tech school you want to get in. We have a few applications and brochures. So whatever you wish to get into and make a career out of, we will pay all of your bills to get you into it. Regardless if it's computers, cars, electronics, nursing, or whatever you want, God has your back. Please understand that it's not us doing this but God doing it through us.

"God is using us to do His goodness, just like Satan misuses us to do his wrong deeds. There are only two things in life, and those are just Christ or Satan, life or death, blessing or cursing, heaven or hell. The only control we have out of those things is our choice of which one we will be serving. So before we became Christians, we were serving Satan, death, cursing, and hell. Now that we are born again, we are serving Jesus, life, blessings, and heaven. We were headed straight to hell. Now we are headed straight to heaven."

All of the Bloods hollered, "Amen and amen!"

Brother T. Moses continued, "That's a word straight from the Lord to all of us. Now, how many of y'all are willing to sign up for a trade tech school so you can get a career going for yourselves?"

They all raised their hands up. While T. Moses was talking, brothers Quin, Derrick, and Donovan were laying out the brochures and applications on five line tables right in front of the pulpit. They helped the Bloods fill out the applications and helped them choose what was best for them.

Meanwhile, Jim Jones and O. G. Van were standing there in awe of what they were seeing and hearing.

O. G. Van said, "I never knew that I was serving Satan."

With tears in his eyes, Jim Jones turned and looked at O. G. Van and said, "Me neither, Cuz, but what that OG Blood said sure made sense, and I believe it. We either serve Jesus Christ or Satan."

They both spoke at the same time and said, "I want to serve Jesus Christ."

The Altadena sheriff chaplain and the Pasadena police chaplain both heard what Jim Jones and O. G. Van said and were touched by what they heard.

The four brothers that were financing the Bloods trade tech schooling came over to Jim Jones and O. G. Van and introduced themselves and told them that they too could sign up and have their pick of any trade tech school and won't have to pay for it. All of the Bloods heard the offer being made to the two Crips, and they all came over to where they were and tried to encourage them to take the offer.

Jim Jones said, "Look, we would love to sign up with y'all, and we appreciate your encouragement, but we would feel as if we were deserting our homeboys back in the hood. They know that we came to meet with a couple of you Bloods to see and hear for ourselves that y'all had sincerely giving your lives to Jesus Christ. For us to go back with some type of accepted offering, no matter how blessed it is, but does not include them might not be received well. Now with that being said, we would ask that offering be held until we talk to our homeboys?"

Brother Quin asked the other three brothers that were making the offer to come together for a moment. While they were talking, the Bloods were all shaking the Crips' hands and introducing themselves and telling them that they understood why they did not accept the offering without their homeboys.

MD said, "As a matter of fact, all of us Bloods accepted the offer together."

Brothers Derrick and Donovan overheard MD, and they said something to Brother Quin and T. Moses, and they shook their heads.

Brother Donovan walked up to Jim Jones and O. G. Van and said, "We feel your situation, and we stand in agreement with y'all. So we are extending God's blessed offering not only to you two but to your whole hood, if they will accept it."

O. G. Van said, "Man, what did we do to deserve this?"

Brother Derrick said, "You did not do anything to deserve it. That's just the way God loves us. We did not do anything to deserve to go to heaven but God has blessed us so."

Jim Jones said, "We will tell our homeboys exactly what we have seen and heard here today and that we believe that the Pasadena Denver Lane Blood Gang are now Christians."

The next day, the church in the Crips' hood were preparing to walk their final laps around the Crips' projects. All of the church members were pulling up in the church's parking lot, and they were also walking up, coming from the projects, as some of the church members lived in the projects themselves. While they were all gathering outside of the church, the pastor was inside talking to the Altadena sheriff chaplain. The chaplain explained what happened at the church in the Bloods' hood yesterday with the job offering to the Bloods, as well as the Crips being offered the same blessing.

The pastor was just amazed at what he heard. Then the phone rang, and the pastor answered it. As he was speaking, they could hear the excitement in his voice. He ended the phone conversation with, "Thank you. We will be waiting."

When he hung up the phone, he turned to the chaplain and said, "That was the pastor from the Pasadena church, and the Bloods were there too. They want to come up and make the final march with us. Even the Bloods are coming with their whole church."

So they went out to the parking lot to tell everyone that the Pasadena church was coming up with all of the Bloods to walk the final laps with them.

The whole parking lot hollered, "Amen!"

12

CHAPTER

Meanwhile, the Crips were all in back of the projects listening to Jim Jones and O. G. Van, telling them that the Bloods were truly born-again Christians and that they saw with their own eyes every one of the Bloods praising Jesus Christ as Lord of their lives.

One of the Crips asked, "How do you feel about that, Cuz?"

Jim Jones answered, "Actually, I felt jealous. I was envying them dudes. Here we were, two Crips in the midst of over a hundred or so Bloods, and all they were doing was showing us respect and love. They were trying to share their blessings with us."

Rick-Rock asked, "What do you mean share their blessings?"

Jim Jones said, "Four ex-Blood gang members were blessed with their own businesses, and they offered every Blood member a chance to go to any trade tech school that they wanted to go to, and it would be paid in full. Then they offered it to O. G. Van and myself. All of the Bloods surrounded us were trying to encourage us to share in their blessings."

Con Man asked, "So what did y'all do, Cuz?"

O. G. Van said, "We turned them down."

Mad Man said, "Y'all turned down someone that was going to pay for y'all to go to any trade tech school. Why?"

O. G. Van looked at Jim Jones, and with tears in his eyes, Jim Jones said, "We did not want to do anything without y'all, Cuz. We felt like we would have been shaking y'all."

Killa Martin said, "Cuz, we really appreciate y'all, but maybe you should have taken them up on their offer."

Jim Jones said, "Well, it worked out for the better, Cuz. Now those same OG Bloods have extended their offer to all of us Crips."

Everyone fell silent. O. G. Van broke the silence and said, "Now, what y'all want to do? Y'all said we should have taken that offer, but when that same offer is presented to y'all, you seem to be stuck. Well, just so you know, ain't no one ever offered me a chance to do something legit and pay my way too. Now that I know y'all have the same opportunity as I do, I do not feel as if I'm leaving y'all behind. Y'all all know the things I've been through since that shooting." As tears rolled down his face, he continued, "I'm getting an education."

Jim Jones said, "Me too, Cuz."

One by one, all of the Crips said that they were going to accept the offer.

By this time, the Pasadena church had pulled up into the Altadena church's parking lot. All of the Bloods pulled up first. They were in two church buses and also in their own cars. The Altadena church members just started clapping when they saw a sea of red-clothed men coming off from the buses. Then the Pasadena church members started pulling up in car loads. The whole parking lot was filled up, and the street's parking spaces were taken up as well.

They all knew what time it was, and they all knew exactly what to do. The Altadena church all started lining up to start the march of seven laps around the projects. This was to be the last day of their march of reclamation of the Crips and their projects from Satan's grasp.

As the Altadena church started filing out of the parking lot, headed straight to the projects, the Pasadena church and the Bloods fell right in behind them, all lined up in twos. It had to be at least a thousand people. Two lines of five hundred long with the Bloods bringing up the rear, all dressed in red.

Some of the neighbors outside of the church and projects called Altadena sheriff's station, complaining about the crowd and the noise of the choir singing. The Altadena sheriff's gang task force were already told by the chaplain of their station about the march of the church around the projects. After receiving the call from a complaining neighbor, the task force decided to go take a look. When they got to the projects and saw how many people were involved in the march, they were surprised, especially when they saw all of them

Bloods dressed in their red gang colors, bringing up the rear of the march.

One of the task force officers pulled out his cell phone and called the task force unit in Pasadena and asked their sergeant if he knew that the Bloods were up there marching around the projects in the Crips' hood with the churches.

The Pasadena task force sergeant said that he did not know that the Bloods were up their marching around the projects. He also said that he and his officers were coming up there to see it for themselves.

By that time, the churches had already walked two of the seven laps around the Crips' hood. Then the Bloods made eye contact with the Altadena task force, who were looking at them with malice and unbelief.

Both chaplains from the Altadena and Pasadena stations were walking with the Bloods, and they did not appreciate those officers being there. By the time they walked two or more laps around projects, the other task force officers from Pasadena showed up and was standing with the Altadena sheriff's task force.

The chaplains did not say anything because the march called for silence (except for the singers and prayers and the reading of the Word). The Bloods just looked at the officers and shook their heads, knowing that those officers were over there hating.

One of the officers asked the other officers if they noticed the bright light over the Crips' hood and also, if they noticed that that the same light was not over the outside of the projects.

One of the Altadena task force officers said, "It's been like that for a week or so."

One of the Pasadena task force officers said, "That same light is over the Bloods' hood too."

Just as quickly as they said what they saw and noticed the light, they dismissed it as if they never did notice it. The devil would not let them understand the Spirit of the Lord moving on those Crips and Bloods.

Those officers could not understand the things of the Spirit because they are not of the Spirit. All those officers could think about where the murders of those two little kids and that one of those Bloods and one of those Crips had to pay for it. Those officers wanted to walk into the projects and catch the Crips off guard, but the Holy Spirit would not let them go into the projects because a great movement was about to take place.

The churches had three more laps to go to make it seven, which would compete their mission to the Lord. The Crips heard the choir outside of their projects, and once again, they saw the brightness of the light getting brighter and brighter over their hood with each lap that the churches were making around their hood.

The Crips all walked to the front of the projects, and when they saw how many people were walking in twos right alongside each other, it blew their minds. Then when they saw the Bloods, all dressed in red, bringing up the rear, walking in twos right along with the churches, they knew that only God could be doing this.

Jim Jones saw the four OG Bloods who made the offer to pay for their educations, so he pointed them out to the rest of the Crips and told them that those were the ones who made the offer to pay for their educations. No one in the line said anything to the Crips for they were allowing the Holy Spirit to have His way with them.

As the end of the line went by the Crips, the task force officers were in clear sight, across the street from the projects, facing the Crips. The Crips just looked at them and automatically knew that those officers were over there hating the fact that someone was trying to help the Crips and Bloods.

O. G. Van said, "Cuz, I do not know about y'all, but I'm getting in that line the next time it comes around. Y'all said that y'all was going to accept their offer of paying for our schooling. Well, those OG Bloods said some words about us having a choice to serve Jesus Christ or Satan, good or evil, blessing or cursing, life or death, which would determine whether we go to heaven or hell."

Jim Jones said, "Yeah, Cuz, that was pretty deep too."

Money Mike asked, "What are y'all talking about, Cuz?"

Jim Jones said, "They were saying that there are only two things in life, and those two things are Jesus Christ or Satan, good or evil, life or death. Whom we serve is up to us."

Mad Man said, "So with the wrong things that we have been doing, we must have been serving Satan."

O. G. Van said, "That's exactly right, Cuz."

With tears in his eyes, O. G. Van continued, "Who else would kill a child?"

Con Man said, "But you did not mean to kill that kid, Cuz."

O. G. Van said, "Yet the child was still killed. That shows us right there that we were being controlled by Satan. I cannot explain it any better than that, but something tells me that y'all know exactly what I'm saying."

By this time, the church was coming around the corner, and as they passed by the Crips, they did not look at them for they were staying focused on their march, and they felt the Spirit of the Lord working on the Crips.

As the end of the line was going by, O. G. Van and Jim Jones fell right in line behind the Bloods. Two by two, the rest of the Crips fell in line behind their homeboys.

Every one of the Crips fell in line, about a hundred of them, all dressed in blue. What a sight to see—the Bloods all dressed in red (their gang colors) and the Crips all dressed in blue (their gang colors) following the churches from their respective hoods.

There was only one more lap to go, and the Crips just walked in silence, in twos. As they fell in line behind the Bloods, the task force officers actually thought that the Crips were about to make a move on the Bloods, but to their surprise, they were merely getting in line.

As they were completing the laps, a few of the Crips and the Bloods had tears rolling down their faces. The task force officers had so much hate for the Crips and the Bloods that they were trying to figure out a way to sabotage this movement.

Narrator

Satan knew that he could not use the Crips and the Bloods right then, so he was trying to use the task force officers to try and break up what God had put together between the Crips and Bloods.

*****

When the churches completed their last lap, the church members just all started clapping and speaking in tongues. They marched into the projects, and the light of the Lord was so bright that one could not help but tell that God was there revealing Himself.

As they got to the back of the projects, the church realized for the first time that the Crips had marched the last lap with them. They surrounded the Crips and Bloods. It looked like a riot was about to take place between the Crips and the Bloods and the churches were the instigators. The only difference was that the churches and even the Bloods were instigating the Crips to become Christians.

The pastor of the Altadena church asked for silence as he approached the Crips.

Me-Ma was holding O. G. Van's and Jim Jones's hands, and Ayo was standing next to O. G. Van.

The pastor asked, "Do you gentlemen know who is holding your hands?"

Jim Jones answered, "Of course, we do."

The pastor asked O. G. Van if he knew who was holding his hand. O. G. Van just shook his head yes because he could not speak without breaking down.

Mommu (the mother of the little boy killed in the Bloods' hood) was standing there holding the hands of MD and D-Rock.

The pastor of the Pasadena church asked MD and D-Rock if they knew who was holding their hands.

D-Rock spoke up, "Yes, we know who she is. We call her Mommu."

The pastor looked at MD and asked him, "Do you know who she is?"

MD, just like O. G. Van, could not speak. He just nodded his head yes with tears coming down his face.

Now neither of the mothers of the slain children knew that they were holding the hands of the actual shooters of their children. But God knew, and so did O. G. Van and MD, and their homeboys knew that it was them that killed those kids.

Narrator

God allowed the heavy burdens that were already on their hearts and in their conscience to attack their souls with the darts of conviction. God's ministering angels (the OG Bloods telling them that there were only two things in life—Jesus Christ or Satan, heaven or hell) told them of God's judgments so that they will understand their sense of need, that they might cry out, "What must I do to be saved."

*****

Now both mothers (Me-Ma and Mommu) had already forgiven the shooters of their children even though they never met them (as far as they knew anyway). The mothers were devout Christians who sincerely believe and know that their children are in heaven with God and Jesus Christ and would rather that their children be in heaven in complete peace, joy, and comfort than here on this earth.

The pastor from the Pasadena church said, "We will let Me-Ma and Mommu speak to y'all. They both sacrificed their children for this movement, hoping that both of you Crips and Bloods would become Christians and go to heaven with us."

Mommu whispered into the pastor's ear that they might not be able to speak loud enough for everyone to hear. The pastor that she whispered to was from the Pasadena church, but they were in Altadena, so he asked the pastor from the Altadena church if they could all go over to his church, and he said, "Of course."

So the pastor from the Altadena church had his congregation form a four-by-four line in front of the Crips and Bloods while the pastor from the Pasadena church had his congregation form a four-by-four line behind the Crips and Bloods.

Once the lines were formed, the pastor of the Altadena church said, "Let us march over to our church so that what needs to be said by Mommu and Me-Ma can be heard by all."

The pastors strategically put the Crips and Bloods between the two churches so that none of them would slip away. As they started walking out of the projects, the task force officers were still out there,

100

as if they were stuck. The Pasadena and the Altadena sheriff and police chaplains of those stations saw them still out there in front of the projects and were disturbed that they were still there.

Narrator

There were demons hovering over the officers' heads, waiting for an opportunity to send those officers on a destructive mission.

*****

As their marchers entered the church, the Pasadena church members and the Bloods all sat on the left side of the church and all of the Altadena church members and the Crips sat on the right side of the church. The Bloods were seated in the front on their side. Mommu and Me-Ma and the chaplains from the police and sheriff stations and the pastors from both churches all walked up onto the podium where the preaching was done at.

After everyone sat down, the pastor of that Altadena church asked everyone to bow their heads for a prayer. When he finished praying, he called Me-Ma and Mommu and gave them both microphones and told them to say what God had put on their hearts.

Narrator

The Lord had the full attention of the Bloods and the Crips for they knew that those were the mothers of the children that were killed by their homeboys. The Crips and the Bloods felt so convicted sitting there, looking at those two mothers. In the process of that feeling of conviction, they also felt God holding them. God is not a respecter of persons, but He is the God of all comfort.

*****

Me-Ma (the mother of the slain little girl that was killed by the Crips) started speaking first. She said, "First of all, we want to let both of you Crips and Bloods know that we forgive y'all for allowing yourselves to be misused by Satan. It was the devil's spirit that misled y'all to try and kill each other and everybody in between y'all. Which, at one time, happened to be our little boy and girl. You see, the devil figured first to use your bullets to kill our children, then he could still have continue to misuse y'all to do more killing. Regardless if it be yourselves or someone not even involved in gangs. The devil does not care which one of y'all, us, or our children would die. Just as long as some killing is going on. The devil does not want y'all to go to heaven or anyone else for that matter.

"He is here to steal, kill, and destroy, but Jesus Christ came that we might have life and have it more abundantly. When I heard that all of you Bloods had given your lives to Jesus Christ, the Holy Spirit shot up in my bones, and I immediately had Jim Jones go and get all of the Crips and bring them to my place so I could tell them how God moved on you Bloods to give your lives to Jesus Christ.

"Now look at you all, sitting here giving God your full attention. God wants you all to know that he loves you and forgives you all for everything that you've ever done. And I do mean everything—from murder to mayhem—whatever. God forgives you, and so do we. You do not even have to worry about paying for your past crimes and sins because Jesus Christ has already paid for them in full. It is Satan, the accuser, who wants to lock you up forever or kill you, then after that, he wants to see you all in hell. But God has already sent His Son, Jesus Christ, to prison for you to be killed for you, then after that, He went to hell for you.

"When Jesus Christ went to hell for us, He took back the authority that man [Adam and Eve] gave Satan. Now that Jesus Christ has the keys to life, heaven, and hell, it's our choice if we want heaven or hell, life or death, blessings or cursing, Jesus Christ or Satan. The choice is ours.

"Jesus Christ paid the penalty for every sin you or I have ever committed. Our debt has been paid in full. If you choose Jesus Christ as Lord of your life, you are not guilty and you are completely forgiven, as if you never did sin. Not only does God forgive you, but we forgive you too. Mommu and I forgive you for the shootings of our children. You see, we know for a fact that both of the shooters are in here right now. We know because this whole march that we just completed was done in honor of those shootings. That's right, I said in honor of those shootings. If you choose Jesus Christ as Lord of your lives, when you get to heaven, our son and daughter will probably run up to y'all and hug and kiss y'all and then blow your minds by telling, 'Thank you for sending us to heaven.'

"You see, Satan meant for those killings to bring about more evil and hate, but God meant it for good to come about so that many should live. Listen closely now, take a look at this church service filled up with Crips and Bloods hearing the Word of God. Now think about this, if those bullets would have hit one of you Crips or Bloods, instead of our children, this setting would not have happened. Instead, y'all would be out there killing each other. But God knew that Mommu and I are real Christians and that we would appreciate the fact that our children are in heaven with Him. There is no better place to be than in heaven with the Father God and His Son, Jesus Christ.

"We want the best for our children, so Mommu and myself, just as our kids will when you get to heaven, we thank you for sending our children to heaven, where they are in full peace, joy, and comfort. We mean that with all our hearts. Now do you believe that we forgive you? We do not want you to be locked up in prison for the rest of your life with Satan and his demons. We want y'all to repent and give your lives to Jesus Christ so that we can all live in that same peace, joy, and comfort that our children are expecting in heaven right now."

O. G. Van and MD (the actual shooters of their children) were just standing there, tears ran down their faces.

Me-Ma said, "Now Mommu would like to say a few words to y'all straight from God." Before she gave Mommu the mic, she said, "Now remember, we love you all." As tears rolling down her pretty face, she handed the mic to Mommu.

Mommu said, "I just wanted to let you all know that I stand in full agreement with everything that Me-Ma has said up here. We really do forgive y'all sincerely and completely. So much so that you do not even have to worry about police arresting you for murder. We believe and know that our children are chilling in heaven. These tears that you see are tears of the Holy Spirit, and it's for you that He grieves.

"Please give your lives to Jesus Christ, and He will take away all of your past sins and throw them so far away that it will be as if you never did them. All of the Bloods have already give their lives to Jesus Christ. Now God wants all of you Crips to give your lives to His Son, Jesus Christ, and we will all be a one big happy family. It's that simple. Jesus Christ has done the hard part for us.

"We could not have done what Jesus Christ did in order for us to get to heaven. He has made away for us, but we have to receive it."

She looked at the pastor of the Altadena church and asked him to please come and make an altar call because she felt their spirit ready to receive the Lord.

The pastor grabbed the mic and said, "I can feel their spirit too, Mommu."

He faced the Crips and told them that his spirit was bearing witness with their spirit and that they were ready to receive Jesus Christ as Lord of their lives. He went on to say, "The Lord is calling you right now. He is knocking at the door of your hearts to let Him come into your lives and bless you with His Spirit. All you have to do is confess with your mouths and believe in your hearts that Jesus Christ is Lord and that He died for your sins and that God raised Him from the dead three days later and that you might have everlasting life. All of you who want to accept Jesus Christ as Lord of your lives, please step forward and repeat after me, and you will be saved."

O. G. Van and Jim Jones did not hesitate to walk down to the altar, but the rest of the Crips were hesitating. Two of the Bloods that had already given their lives to the Lord felt that it would encourage the rest of the Crips if they walked down to the altar too. It was MD and D-Rock. When the rest of the Bloods saw their homeboys go down to the altar, they stood up and extended their hands toward the rest of the Crips, encouraging them to walk down the altar.

The rest of the Crips all started walking down to the altar, and the Bloods were acting as their escorts. Me-Ma and Mommu were simply blessed to see such a beautiful sight.

The pastor said, "Praise God, praise God. Now repeat after me, and you will be saved."

As he said the prayer of salvation, all of the Crips repeated after him, and so did the Bloods too, just to show support for they were already saved.

Narrator

Because the Crips humbled themselves once before to escort those ladies to church, the Lord had them escorted to the altar by the Bloods. They were reaping the goodness that they sowed.

Satan, himself, came up and started slapping demons around because he was so mad at them for losing the Crips and Bloods. While he was slapping them around, he looked over to the task force officers and the demons that he had assigned to them hovering over the officers. They waved for him to come over to where they were so they could make a plan to use those officers to attack the Crips and the Bloods.

*****

After the Crips and the Bloods received the Lord Jesus Christ as their Savior, the pastor said a prayer of thanks to God for honoring the churches' obedience of His call on them to march around the Crips' and the Bloods' hoods. He also prayed for God to fill the Crips and the Bloods with His Holy Spirit and the power of discernment so that they would know when Satan was trying to attack them.

After he said, "In Jesus's name, amen!" the Crips and the Bloods hugged each other and started apologizing for all of the wrongdoings that they had done to each other. While the Crips and the Bloods were doing that, the pastors and the chaplains walked over to Me-Ma and Mommu and hugged them and told them that God was awesome, and they thanked them for allowing them to be a part of their Christian lives.

Me-Ma grabbed the mic and asked for everyone's attention. Everyone got quiet and she said, "Welcome to the family of God. You Crips and Bloods have become a part of the body of Christ. Mommu and I have invested our children to the Lord, and now we have many more children in you all."

All of the Crips and the Bloods started clapping and pumping their fists in the air. The four ex-Blood gang members that were going to pay for all of the Crips' and Bloods' education came up on the stage, and they were handed the microphone.

Brother T. Moses said, "God bless you, brothers. Now we have an offer for all of you Crips. It's the same offer that we made to the Bloods, which they all accepted. My name is T. Moses. This is Brother Quin, Brother Donovan, and Brother Derrick. We are all ex-Blood gang members, and God has blessed us with successful businesses, and we wish to now bless you all with a chance to go to any trade tech school you wish to go to, and we will pay for it in full. The Bloods have already signed up for it. Now it's your turn, if you want it."

The Bloods were encouraging all of the Crips to get hooked up, so all of the Crips stepped forward. Brothers Quin, Derrick, and Donovan started opening up briefcases and started passing out brochures and applications. The Bloods were helping the Crips fill out the forms. It was the most amazing sight to see.

After they filled out all the forms and turned them in, Brother T. Moses told them that they would be getting their class schedules in the mail within three weeks.

Jim Jones said, "We thank you, brothers, for caring enough about us to do something so major in our lives."

Tears just started rolling down Jim Jones's face when Brother Quin jumped off the podium and hugged him and told him, "God is the one who gets all of the thanks and glory."

All of the Crips and the Bloods hollered in unison, "Thank You, Lord."

The pastor never heard anything so loud in his church before.

While all of that was taking place on the church floor, Mommu and Me-Ma were on the stage where they had spoken from, talking to each other about how God had blessed them with all of these young men in return for their son and daughter. Mommu told Me-Ma, "We must keep our hands on them so that Satan does not steal them back."

The pastor of the Pasadena church walked up to them and asked if everything was okay. They told him that they were thinking of ways to keep the Crips' and the Bloods' minds on Jesus Christ. Me-Ma asked if he and the rest of the chaplains would come over to her place the next day for lunch so that they could pray for God to give them the wisdom on what to do to keep the minds of the Crips and the Bloods on His Son, Jesus Christ. They all agreed to meet at her place the next day.

The pastor of the Altadena church told everyone to go tell their families that they have accepted Jesus Christ as Lord of their lives. He also told them that it would bless them to apologize to anyone that they may had offended in the past. They were also told to report to the church the following Sunday.

As they were walking out of the church, Jim Jones and MD were talking about hooking up a barbecue for both the Crips and Bloods to attend.

The task force officers were still out there sitting on their cars. It had to be at least two-and-a-half hours that they were out there, stuck on hate.

Narrator

Satan and his demons were lurking right over the officers, and when the Crips and the Bloods, along with the church members all came out of the church, Satan and his demons and even the cops all just stopped what they were doing and just stared at the church movement. Satan was seething with rage.

*****

The police chaplains who saw those officers still hanging out there said to each other that they would keep an eye on them. They also agreed to go talk to them right then. As they approached the officers, the demons in the atmosphere were going crazy, wanting the officers to attack the chaplains.

The Pasadena chaplain told the officers from his station that the Crips had given their lives to Jesus Christ, just as the Bloods did the other day.

The task force sergeant said, "We will see about that."

The chaplains just shook their heads at the officers and walked away. As they were walking away, they looked at each other, letting the other know that they saw the hatred and evil in those officers' eyes.

The next day, the pastors and the two chaplains all met at Me-Ma's apartment to talk and pray for God to give them the wisdom to direct the Crips' and Bloods' attention span to stay on Jesus Christ. But before they could even pray, God had already answered their prayers. There was a knock on Me-Ma's door. Mommu looked at Me-Ma for their spirits was bearing witness of God's Spirit moving at the knock of that door.

Me-Ma just hollered, "Come in."

When the door opened, it was Jim Jones, O. G. Van, MD, and D-Rock.

The pastors and the chaplains said, "What a blessing to see you all rolling together, Crips and Bloods."

Jim Jones said, "We are no longer enemies. We are brothers in Christ Jesus."

Me-Ma said, "We were just about to pray for God to give us the wisdom to keep your minds on His Son, Jesus Christ."

D-Rock said, "That's basically why we came here, to ask y'all to come to our barbecue this weekend that we are giving at Loma Alta Park. Next weekend, we will be having another one at the Jackie Robinson Center in Pasadena. We figured that if we do things together, we would become closer and our minds will not be on the old things they used to be on."

The pastor from the Altadena church asked, "Who is paying for these barbecues?"

O. G. Van said, "We used to just go to the market and steal all of the meat and beer that we wanted, but now, we know that's not God's way, so we will be bringing food from our homes. Of course, we will not be drinking beer, so we will be trying to come up on some sodas."

The pastor said, "Do not worry about the food and drinks because the church will pay for it."

The other pastor said, "And we will pay for the following barbecue at the Jackie Robinson Center next weekend."

Me-Ma and Mommu said that they wanted to do all of the cooking at both barbecues.

Mommu said, "We want you Crips and Bloods to know that we feel that God has blessed us with all of you as our children because we sincerely gave our daughter and son in those shootings that Satan had your gangs doing."

Me-Ma spoke up, "Yeah, the devil did not expect us to respond in love and forgiveness. The devil wanted us to hate y'all and have you all locked up in prison for life, where he could really have you to himself, but God knew our hearts belonged to Him and that we would gladly send Him our children, and because of our obedience to love instead of hate, God has blessed us with all of you Crips and Bloods."

O. G. Van, the actual shooter of Me-Ma's daughter, just started shedding tears. When MD, the actual shooter of Mommu's son, saw those tears of O. G. Van's, he too started shedding tears. O. G. Van and MD did not know that they were the respective ones that shot the kid in each other's hood. They just knew about themselves being the shooter. But it dawned on Me-Ma and Mommu that every time they mentioned the forgiveness of the shooters of their children, these two in particular started crying.

Me-Ma said, "You two shedding those tears, come right over here and sit next to me for a moment."

When they came to sit by Me-Ma, Mommu said, "Praise God" for the Lord had just revealed to her that these two were the shooters that Satan misused to shoot their children.

Me-Ma said, "Now I do not want y'all to say a word until God is finished speaking through me to y'all."

They just shook their heads okay. With humility, they both just sat there with their heads bowed, listening intently to what Me-Ma was about say.

Mommu said, "Before she speaks, I want y'all to know that I stand in full agreement with what God says to you two through her. Just like Satan misused y'all to do, God will say the good He wants done on earth."

She then looked at Me-Ma and said, "Go ahead, sister, and let them know and hear what kind of God we serve."

Me-Ma said, "Now remember that this is God speaking, not us, but we do stand in full agreement with whatever God is going to say. The Holy Spirit has revealed to us exactly who you two were and what you two have done."

MD and O. G. Van looked at Mommu and Me-Ma to see if they could tell if she was serious or just finishing. When they looked up into Me-Ma's and Mommu's eyes, the Holy Spirit revealed to MD and O. G. Van themselves that God knew and that He did in fact reveal it to both mothers exactly who they were.

The Holy Spirit even revealed to them the word *were*, as in who they *were*, and not who they *are* now, which in turn, comforted them to let down any guards that they might have had.

Narrator

God had set the stage for MD and O. G. Van to have their hearts softened and ready to hear, understand, and receive true forgiveness.

*****

Me-Ma continued, "Every time we talk about our kids going to heaven to be with the Lord or how we forgive their shooters, you two start shedding tears of sincere remorsefulness. The Holy Spirit has revealed it to Mommu and to me that you two *were* the shooters. Do not speak. Let God finish saying what He has to say to you two. You see, the operative word in that statement is *were*.

"That's not who you *are* now. Can you hear and understand the difference in that? *Were* and *are*? You *were* the ones that Satan misused to shoot our children. But now, you *are* born-again Christians, children of God. Who you *are* now erases all of the past deeds and sins done in the spirit of Satan, who misused your willing vessels.

"Being born again means that you have no past. When a baby is born into this world, you can't walk up to that baby, who is only an hour old, and say that baby shot me two hours ago. When in fact, the baby was only born an hour ago. He was not in existence two hours ago. So that's how it is with you two. To God and us, you do not have a past. Old things have passed away. All things have become new.

"God forgives you, and so do we. Jesus Christ has paid for your past sins, so you do not have to. Now that's not to say that the people of this world forgives you. They will still accuse you and try to lock you up to make you pay for your crimes and your sins. But we are your family now, and we forgive you, just like God forgives you. So we are not going to turn you in to the police. Even if we did turn you in now, we would be turning in the wrong people because those two who shot our children do not exist anymore."

O. G. Van and MD were just humbly sitting there as tears ran down their faces. Jim Jones and D-Rock got up out of their seats and went and stood behind their homeboys, trying to give them strength. Mommu got up out of her seat and sat down right between MD and O. G. Van.

They looked at Mommu and said, "We are so sorry, and we do not deserve the love that you two are showing us."

Then they looked at Me-Ma, who had done most of the talking, and said to her, "We are so sorry, Me-Ma, so, so sorry."

She said, "We know that you two born-again Christians are remorseful, and that's how we knew that you two *were* the shooters without y'all telling us. We saw and felt your sorrow, and the Holy

Spirit confirmed it to us with His discerning gift on us. We only have one question for you two. Will y'all be our spiritual children?"

They said, "Of course, we will. It would be our honor."

Jim Jones and D-Rock said, "Can we be your spiritual children too?"

They all laughed and hugged each other as Me-Ma and Mommu answered, "Of course, y'all can. As a matter of fact, we feel that for all of your homeboys too. Make sure that y'all tell them that too."

MD and O. G. Van looked at the chaplains of the police and sheriff departments for they were still cops too. The chaplains knew exactly what they were thinking, and so to set them at ease, they told them not to worry about them turning them in or ever mentioning it to anyone.

The Altadena sheriff chaplain took it a little further by saying, "We are Christians first and foremost, and we stand in full agreement with this God movement. Plus, we never heard y'all say that you did it. All we heard was Me-Ma said that God has revealed it to them. Y'all said that you were sorry, but you never did say what you were sorry for. So you never admitted anything in front of us. So this is what we are going to do, we are going to leave y'all here with the pastors and Me-Ma and Mommu to let y'all finish talking, but I will leave y'all with this. After y'all leave here today, don't ever mention what y'all talked about here today ever again. Leave it in God's hands, okay?"

The two chaplains hugged Me-Ma and Mommu and told them that they loved them and that they are the truest Christians that they ever did see. As tears ran down the chaplains' faces, they hugged the pastors and all of the Crips and Bloods and walked out.

The pastor from the Altadena church in Crips' hood said, "Okay, now we are going to straighten all of this out and leave it right here in God's hands."

Me-Ma said, "Listen, it's already straightened out with us. We forgive them. It's now forgiven."

MD said, "Well, Me-Ma and Mommu, there is something else that needs to be straightened out between us Bloods and Crips about those shootings. First of all, we are truly humbled by your forgiveness and never have we ever seen or felt the love of God that you two spiritual mothers have and are showing us. I want to confess to you first, Mommu"—as tears were rolling down his face—"that it was my bullet that hit and killed your son. I was shooting at the Crips, but one of the bullets strayed and hit your son. We blamed it on the Crips in order to keep the blame off from us."

Then he looked at O. G. Van and Jim Jones and apologized to them for making them think that they had killed a little boy.

Jim Jones told MD, "Do not even worry about it. We also have something to confess." Jim Jones looked at O. G. Van, who was sitting on the couch with his head bowed down, and asked him if he wanted to speak or should he do it for him.

O. G. Van picked his head up and said, "Naw, I need to do this myself." He got up and said, "Me-Ma, the Bloods did not kill your daughter in that drive-by. It was my bullet that went astray as I was trying to shoot the Bloods. We also blamed it on the Bloods to keep the heat off from us." He then looked at MD and D-Rock and asked them to please forgive him and his hood for blaming them for that shooting.

D-Rock said, "That goes without saying, especially now that we are all born-again Christians."

O. G. Van looked at Me-Ma and Mommu and said, "We do not know the words to say to you two beautiful spiritual mothers, but we are truly sorry."

Me-Ma said, "Y'all do not have to say anything to us about that stuff. It's all over with, and plus, we put it in God's hands, and that is where we are leaving it. It's over and done away with. So let's do like the chaplain said and never mention it again. Can we all agree on that right now?"

Everyone said, "We agree on that."

The pastor said, "You gentlemen have just received the grace and mercy of God. Please always respect that gift of new life that you've been given."

Me-Ma and Mommu got up out of their seats and extended their arms out to MD and O. G. Van to hug them and tell them that they love them in a real way.

After they hugged them two, Jim Jones and D-Rock said, "We want a hug too."

They all laughed, and hugs went around for everyone.

As the two chaplains left, they were talking to each other about what they had just heard.

The Altadena sheriff chaplain said, "I pray that those two boys leave that in God's hand and never mention it again."

The Pasadena police chaplain said, "I believe that they will not mention it again. Especially, after they have been given a new lease on life because of the shootings. We must make sure that task force officers do not find out about what went down."

When the chaplains went back to their respective stations to return their station vehicles and change into their personal clothes, the Altadena chaplain overheard the task force officers plotting to do something to make the Crips and the Bloods hate each other again. The Pasadena chaplain also overheard his station's task force officers talking about coming up with a plan to have the Crips and the Bloods back at war with each other. Neither group knew that the chaplains were overhearing them. Both chaplains felt that the hand of God placed them there to hear what Satan was trying to do through those officers.

Narrator

Satan was going to try and misuse those officers to bring about destroying what God had done with the Crips and Blood. Those officers did not know that they were being misused, blinded by Satan himself.

*****

The Pasadena police task force sergeant told his officers, "Out of all of those Crips and Bloods that were in that church in Altadena, two of them are the shooters of those two kids. I cannot understand how the mothers of those children were there acting as if nothing happened. Well, we are not going to let them get away with it."

He looked at his officers and asked them, "How many of you are with me in stirring up this mess?"

They all raised their hands. The sergeant said, "Okay, here is what we are going to do."

Their police chaplain was right on the other side of their lockers, listening to their whole conversation, but they did not know it. So the sergeant kept on talking. He said, "We are going to the impound to get a car and grab some red rags to cover our faces up and use some guns out of the evidence room to go and do a drive-by on the Crips tomorrow night. They will think that it's the Bloods, and when they retaliate, the war will be back on, and then we can get to the bottom of these two child killings. I'm going to call the Altadena task force sergeant and let them know what's up. Maybe they will do the same thing with some blue rags covering their face and shoot at the Bloods. As a matter of fact, they might be willing to do the so-called retaliation on the Bloods after we do the drive-by on the Crips. That will be perfect to get the Crips and Bloods back on the gangbanging trail."

The Pasadena police chaplain could not believe what he was hearing. He could not wait to call the Altadena sheriff chaplain and let him know what the task force officers were planning to try to break up what God had done. The Pasadena chaplain called the Altadena sheriff chaplain. He said that he was also listening to the task force officers from his station, and they were in their locker room when he overheard a phone call with the task force sergeant, and it seemed that they had agreed to do something, but he did not hear the whole plan, and they do not know that he overheard them.

So the chaplains agreed to meet each other at Jim's Burgers on Lincoln and Woodberry streets in Altadena.

Meanwhile, the Crips and the Bloods were gathering all their weapons so that they could turn them in to the pastors at their respective churches. The Crips came up with about ninety guns and knives, and the Bloods came up with about the same amount.

Jim Jones called D-Rock and told him what the Crips came up with, and D-Rock told Jim Jones that the Bloods came up with about the same amount. They both agreed to call their pastors and see if they could turn them in to them.

When the pastors got the phone calls from Jim Jones and D-Rock, asking them if they could turn in their weapons, they were moved with blessed joy because the Crips and the Bloods were doing this without being asked to. It showed how committed they were to changing their lives. The pastors could not deny them, so they told them to hold them up because they did not want the Crips and Bloods to get caught riding over to the churches with all of those weapons. The pastors called each other and were overexcited about the Crips and Bloods turning in their weapons, even more so, because they were not asked to do it.

The pastors agreed to call the police and the sheriff chaplains and ask them how they should go about picking up the weapons.

The chaplains told the pastors that they needed to talk to them about what they overheard about the task force officers' plans, but they all agreed that they should pick up those weapons first. So the chaplains went with the pastors to pick up those weapons so that they could figure out a way to dispose them.

The chaplain of the Pasadena police task force went to the church where the Bloods attended and hooked up with the pastor of their church, and they went to the projects to meet with MD and D-Rock. The pastor told MD and D-Rock that they were blessed to be a part of their new lives.

MD asked, "What will be done with these weapons?" He asked that question because the gun that shot that little boy was in there and plus, the chaplain was a cop.

The pastor said, "The chaplain is going to take every one of those guns to be melted, and they will never be seen or used again."

The chaplain of the Altadena task force officers went to the church where the Crips attended and met with their pastor, and they went to the projects to meet with Jim Jones and O. G. Van. The pastor told them that he was blessed to see them obeying the Holy Spirit by turning in their weapons.

When O. G. Van saw the sheriff chaplain, he asked, "What would be done with these weapons?" He wanted to know because the gun that killed that little girl was in there.

The chaplain told him that those weapons will be melted and destroyed, never to be used or seen again.

The Crips said, "Please take them away from us."

As the pastors and chaplains met at the place that would be melting the weapons, before they took the guns into the place, they prayed a prayer of thanks to God for using them to be able to reclaim the Crips and the Bloods and their neighborhoods.

After they saw the weapons being destroyed with their own eyes, they left to go and talk. That's when the chaplains told the pastors that they overheard the task force officers from both stations talking about doing drive-by shootings on the Crips and Bloods to try and turn them back against each other. All because they were mad that the Crips and Bloods had gotten free pass on their past.

The pastors asked the chaplains what could be done to stop the officers' plans.

The Altadena sheriff chaplain said, "If we let them know that we know their plan of attack, then they will not do it. But that will not keep them off the Crips' and Bloods' backs. If we could find a way to let them do it then catch them doing it, we might be able to hold it over their heads so that they would leave the Crips and Bloods alone. They are talking about doing it tomorrow night, so we need to talk to the Crips and Bloods so we can try to set something up to trap those officers. The Crips and Bloods may be able to come up with a plan to set the task force officers up."

So the Pasadena police chaplain and the pastor from the Pasadena church said that they would go talk to the Bloods, and the Altadena sheriff chaplain and the pastor from the Altadena church said they would go talk to the Crips.

*****

Jim Jones and O. G. Van were walking from the store when the pastor and the sheriff chaplain road up on them and asked to speak with them. They stopped walking and asked, "What's up?"

The chaplain said, "First of all, we want y'all to know that the weapons have been melted and destroyed. We watched it with our own eyes. Now we have some disturbing news about the Altadena and the Pasadena task forces."

O. G. Van asked, "What is it?"

The sheriff chaplain said, "I overheard the task force officers talking about doing something to make y'all get back into a war with Bloods. While they were talking, they got a phone call from the Pasadena task force, who seemed to have given them a plan of attack on you both to make y'all think that the war was back on."

Jim Jones asked, "So what's their plan?"

When the chaplain told them about the drive-by shootings that the task force officers were planning to do, dressed up as Crips and Bloods, Jim Jones and O. G. Van were very mad.

Jim Jones said, "We need to let the Bloods know that we ain't tripping like that."

The pastor said, "They are being told right now by their church pastor and the chaplain form the Pasadena police station."

Just as they said that, the Pasadena police chaplain and the pastor from the Pasadena church pulled up on them, and they also had MD and D-Rock with them.

As they got out of the car, MD and D-Rock walked right over to Jim Jones and O. G. Van and said, "Y'all heard, huh?"

As they all hugged each other, Jim Jones said, "Yeah, we heard."

MD asked the chaplains and pastors, "How do we stop this? We do not want to be at war with each other ever again, let alone be at war with the police and the sheriffs."

The Pasadena police chaplain said, "We need to catch them in the act so this can be stopped forever."

D-Rock said, "Let's pray right now for God to give us the wisdom on what to do."

Everybody looked at him with surprise in their eyes.

D-Rock said, "I just felt that in my heart, so we know that it came from God."

They all agreed. The pastors said that they should have been the ones saying that. The chaplains said that God was teaching the Bloods and Crips to depend on Him.

13

CHAPTER

They got in a circle right there on the sidewalk. It was about eight of them, standing in agreement that God would give them the wisdom to stop the task force officers. The Altadena pastor prayed, and as he prayed, God gave Jim Jones their answer.

After the prayer, Jim Jones said, "I was given a vision while you were praying. That has never happened to me before, so I know that it came from God."

The Altadena pastor asked, "What was the vision?"

Jim Jones said, "While you were praying, I saw in my head the Bloods all chilling in their hood, then I saw the Crips all chilling in our Hood, then I saw officers in plain clothes that I never seen before, and they all had on blue windbreakers with the letters IA on the left side of them. Then I saw a car coming with four heads in it, and as they passed by the alley, two vans pulled out behind them flashing red lights to pull them over. Then I saw the same thing in the Bloods' hood. That is the vision I saw in my head."

The Altadena sheriff chaplain said, "That vision was from God, and we know what to do."

Jim Jones asked, "What does IA mean?"

Both police and sheriff chaplains looked at each other, and both spoke at the same time and said, "Internal Affairs. They are the ones who police the police."

The chaplains said that they would be labeled as snitches for going to them, but they did not care because they knew that the vision came straight from God.

The chaplains told the pastors that they must go and talk to the Internal Affairs officers so that they could set up what needed to be done by tomorrow night. Then they turned to Jim Jones and said, "That vision came straight from God, and it will be that vision that will bring those officers down. We will be back in touch with y'all after we talk to the IA officers."

The pastors said that they would take MD and D-Rock back to their hood. The two Bloods and two Crips told the pastors that they never have been in this type of situations before.

MD said, "It feels funny because we would engage with the police in a shoot-out before we gave our lives to Christ, but now that we are born-again Christians, we can literally feel God protecting us not only from the police but also from ourselves as well."

Both pastors said, "Amen, brothers. Amen!"

The Altadena pastor told the Crips and the Bloods, "Make sure that you have your homeboys right there in the hood tomorrow night so that the gang task force would follow through with their false attack. When we hear from the chaplains, we will contact y'all and give you the scoop. Always remember that God is in charge, but we must keep all things in His hands so that He can have His way with it."

The chaplains from both task force stations went to the Internal Affairs office and met with one of their agents. After the chaplains told the agent what they overheard the task force was saying, the agent asked if they think that the task force officers were serious enough to carry the drive-bys out.

Both chaplains said, "No doubt."

The agent went to get his lieutenant and the chaplains explained it all over again to him. The lieutenant was also a born-again Christian, and he felt the Spirit of the Lord moving on him to believe the chaplains and to do something to stop the task force officers. The lieutenant said, "We will put a stop to this move." He then called in twenty agents to set up a sting that would take down the task force officers.

After he explained what was going on to his agents, one of the chaplains told them that they had the Crips and the Bloods ready to post up in their respective hoods so that they could be easy targets for the drive-bys.

The lieutenant said, "We do not plan on letting those officers fire their weapons. If they are willing to do a fake drive-by as Crips and Bloods, they very well may be willing to actually shoot one of those Crips or Bloods. So as soon as they enter their hoods, we will be pulling them over, just like a regular traffic stop. We will not have to wait for them to fire their illegal weapons because they will be in cars from the impound. Plus, they will have unauthorized weapons and the testimonies of you two chaplains is plenty enough of evidence to prosecute and convict. We just have to make sure that we are in position to pull them over."

Meanwhile, the task force officers were setting up the two drive-bys. They had a friend at the impound that would give them a car without having to sign it out and let them bring the car back, as if it never left. They ended up getting two cars. One for the Pasadena Task Force and one for the Altadena Task Force.

The task force officers from Altadena were going to do their drive-by first on the Crips. Then a half hour later, the Pasadena task force officers would go do there drive-by on the Bloods. Both task force offices would be wearing blue and red rags over their faces, as if they were really Crips and Bloods. The task force officers also had those unauthorized weapons to use for the drive-bys. So everything was set up for the next evening.

*****

The chaplains contacted the pastors who in turn contacted the Crips and Bloods and told them that the vision Jim Jones had was about to come to pass tomorrow night. The Crips and Bloods said that they would be posted up as planned.

Jim Joes and O. G. Van went over to Me-Ma's apartment to let her know what was going on. Ayo was there too, as she was staying with Me-Ma ever since O. G. Van and the Crips stopped her ex-boyfriend from beating her. Ayo and O. G. Van were sitting in the kitchen while Jim Jones and Me-Ma were talking in the living room…

"What's on your mind, son? It looks like something is bothering you."

Jim Jones looked at Me-Ma and said, "Tomorrow night, the gang task forces from Altadena and Pasadena are going to attempt a drive-by shooting in both of our hoods, trying to make us think that it's us tripping on each other again, just to start the war against each other all over again."

Me-Ma said what so loudly that O. G. Van and Ayo came out of the kitchen to see what was going on.

Jim Jones continued telling Me-Ma what was happening. When he told her that the chaplains overheard it all, she felt relieved about it, knowing that they would do something to stop it.

O. G. Van said, "It's amazing how God had those chaplains right there listening to every word without the task force officers knowing it."

Me-Ma said, "God watches over His children."

Jim Jones told Me-Ma that they prayed with the chaplains and the pastors, and God gave him a vision during that prayer, and the chaplains said that the vision was God's way of telling them how to deal with this situation.

Me-Ma said, "God will always give you wisdom if you ask for it."

Jim Jones told Me-Ma how it was all going down the next night.

Ayo told them to be careful, and O. G. Van said, "The Internal Affairs agents will not let them get a shot off."

*****

Down in Pasadena, Mommu had MD and D-Rock at her apartment, telling her what was happening too. She told them that she was so proud of them for staying true to God. After she heard it all, she called Me-Ma, and they just rejoiced at how God was using their new family. Mommu told MD and D-Rock that she was talking to Me-Ma up in Altadena and that O. G. Van and Jim Jones were over there telling her the same thing.

MD said, "Tell them that we must get together after this goes down tomorrow night."

Mommu relayed the message to Me-Ma, and they all agreed to hook up after it all went down.

Me-Ma told Mommu that she was going to ask Jim Jones and O. G. Van to spend the night, and Mommu said, "That sounds like a good idea. I'm going to ask D-Rock and MD the same thing."

So they asked them while they were still on the phone with each other, and they all agreed to spend the night. Me-Ma and Mommu said that they feel comforted every time those boys come around them.

O. G. Van, up in Altadena, and MD, down in Pasadena, both said at the same time, "I feel like a new man."

Me-Ma told Mommu what O. G. Van just said, and Mommu told Me-Ma that MD had just said the same exact words.

Me-Ma said, "God is in full control."

They said their goodbyes and hung up.

The next morning, when they woke up to the smell of breakfast cooking at both apartments, MD said, "I never slept so good like this before." Of course, O. G. Van said the same thing at Me-Ma's place.

After they ate breakfast, the chaplains showed up at Me-Ma's and Mommu's apartments. They went to inform them what was taking place. They were blessed to see the Crips and Bloods already over there. After the chaplains heard that Me-Ma and Mommu already knew what was happening, they told them how everything was going to go down.

The Crips and Bloods were to be just standing around in their hoods, like they used to do before they were born again. Then the task force officers would come down the street to do a drive-by in unmarked cars from the impound, but before they could even get their guns out of their car windows, the IA agents would pull them over at gunpoint and arrest them. This would take place in both hoods. First, in the Crips' hood, then a half hour later, in the Bloods' hood.

Me-Ma and Mommu asked if the officers would get any shots off, and they were assured that they would not. Me-Ma and Mommu prayed with both groups before they left their apartments.

Jim Jones and O. G. Van went to round up all of their home-boys, as MD and D-Rock went to do the same in their hood. Both sets agreed to post up and trust the vision that the Lord gave to Jim Jones.

The task force officers went and got the cars they were going to use from their friend at the impound. No one signed the cars out, so it was like the cars never left the impound. The Internal Affairs office had an agent with the chaplains posted up right outside of the impound, so they would know what kind of cars they would use instead of the two they thought they were going to use. So instead of one car a piece, they would have two cars a piece.

The IA agent wrote down the license plates of all four cars and the make of the cars. Then they went and gave that information to the lieutenant of the IA. The lieutenant sent an agent to go arrest the guy at the impound who illegally gave away some cars to the task force officers.

They were to hold the impound worker at the IA station until it was all over with so he could not call anyone and warn them. Although he was ready to cooperate with the IA, they really did not need his cooperation just yet.

Both task forces met with each other to go over their plan. The Pasadena police task force would put red rags over their faces and drive by in the Crips' hood, firing blank bullets over the Crips' heads in two car loads of four officers. Then about a half hour later, the Altadena sheriff task force will do the same thing to the Bloods in their hood. So at 8:00 p.m., the first two car loads would make their move on the Bloods. They will not call each other because they do not want any connections traced to each other during the time of the shootings.

At first, the Altadena task force were going to do the drive-by on the Crips because they were more familiar with their hood, and the Pasadena police was going to do their drive-by on the Bloods because they were more familiar with their hood. But both task forces thought it would be more convincing if the Bloods' task force officers moved on the Crips and the Crips' task force officers moved on the Bloods, as if they were really gangbangers.

Narrator

The task force officers thought it was part of their good planning, deciding not to call each other. But God would not allow the task force officers to call each other so that they could not warn each other about the sting by the IA agents.

*****

The Crips were chilling right in front of their projects. They saw the IA agents strategically placed so they could block in the two car loads of task force officers and drawn down on them. The IA agents had real live bullets, not knowing that the task force officers were using blanks.

Jim Jones called the Crips into a tight circle and told them that he saw all of this in a vision that God gave him while they were praying and for them not to be worried for God was in full control.

They all said, "Amen!"

Meanwhile, down in the Bloods' hood, they were all chilling in the front of their projects, and they saw the IA agents strategically placed in their hood, just like they were in the Crips' officers, and drawn down on them also with live ammo, not knowing that the task force officers were using blank bullets.

Me-Ma and Mommu called each other and vowed to pray in tongues from 8:00 p.m. 'til 9:00 p.m. without telling anybody. They were so proud of the Crips and Bloods.

So the stage was set. The Pasadena task force officers and the Altadena task force officers were at their meeting place, and they shook hands and told each other that they would meet up after they did their drive-bys and dropped off the cars back at the impound.

The Pasadena task force officers took off first. They drove up to Altadena in two car loads of four. As they got closer, they pulled up their red rags over their faces and pulled out their guns. As they turned onto the street where the Crips were kicking it, they saw them all in front of the projects. The task force officers were so focused on the Crips that they didn't see the vans pulling up behind them nor the two vans that were coming right at them from the opposite direction.

As soon as the task force officers put one gun outside of the passenger side window, the two van loads of IA agents put their spotlights on them and blocked their cars. The IA agents jumped out of their vans with guns drawn. The task force officers were in shock and awe, and they threw their hands up in the air, hollering that they were police officers, thinking that the IA agents were regular cops who think that they were real gang members.

The IA lieutenant spoke through a bullhorn, and he treated the task force officers like common criminals, even though he knew that they were police officers.

He called them out of their cars one by one and laid them face down on the ground. By the time he got to the last officer, he had eight officers spread eagled and face down on the ground. The agents searched their cars and came up with six guns.

The lieutenant said, "Cuff all of them."

Once the task force officers realized that it was the Internal Affairs agents that had them, they knew that they had no love coming from them and that someone had to have snitched on them but could not figure out who.

The lieutenant said, "Put them in the vans. Park their cars until we get the other task force officers who should be ready to make their move on the Bloods because it's almost 8:30 p.m., which is their set time to move."

When the task force officers heard that, they thought that it was one of their own officers that snitched on them because the IA lieutenant was speaking of their planned attack as if he was at their meeting himself.

The lieutenant was looking right at them while he was talking. The sergeant of the task force officers, who was also cuffed up, asked if he could speak, and the lieutenant said, "Not right now, but after we stop that other task force from attacking the Bloods, then I will listen to what you have to say."

The sergeant said, "Let me call them to stop them."

The lieutenant said, "That would defeat the whole purpose of us being out here. We want them to attempt the drive-by so that we can have a charge on them, just as we have an attempted drive-by charge on you."

The sergeant said, "Well, just so you don't fire on them, we were using blank bullets, not live rounds."

The lieutenant said, "That's really dangerous, and you as an officer should know better than anyone."

The lieutenant is a Christian too, so he told the sergeant, "Maybe you could see how the devil is messing with you to mess up what God has done with the Crips and Bloods. Just think about it for a minute. What if we, or some other cops, pulled up on your crew actually doing the drive-by with blank bullets and got in a shoot-out with y'all, and all of you got shot or even killed. That's how much the devil cares for you. But God cares enough for you to send us to save you all from Satan's tricks."

Then he slammed the van door shut on them and told the driver to take them to the staging area at the church in Altadena.

The Crips and the pastors and the chaplains went to the church, opened it up, and went into the sanctuary to pray for the other part of the sting to go as smoothly as the first one did. The task force officers in the IA van already apprehended and started to speak on each other about who could have told them, but the task force sergeant told everyone not to speak because the van was probably bugged to hear what they had to say.

Now down in Pasadena, the IA agents heard from their agents in Altadena and were told that the sting went smoothly, and they were also told about the task force officers using blank bullets. So as the second group of task force officers pulled around the corner to do their drive-by, they saw the Bloods just sitting pretty for them. As they got closer, two vans pulled up behind them, but the officers did not notice for all of their attention was on the Bloods. Another two vans was also coming straight at the task force officers just as they were about to put their guns out of the window of their cars to fire upon the Bloods.

The IA agents flashed their lights on the two car loads of officers, who had blue rays over their faces, and the agents jumped out of their vans with guns drawn. The task force officers were hollering that they were officers.

The senior IA agent called out on his bullhorn for the car loads of officers to step out one by one and lay face down on the ground. When he finished ordering them all out, he had eight officers spread eagled and face down on the ground, just like some common criminals.

The agents searched the two cars and found six guns.

One of the task force officers spoke up and said, "We are cops."

The senior agent said, "We know that you are cops, but right now, you are acting like gangbangers, so we are going to treat you as such." He then turned to his agents and said, "Cuff them up and put them in the vans so we can get to the staging area in Altadena."

Two of the agents drove the two cars that the task force officers were using, and they all followed each other up to the church in Altadena.

MD called Jim Jones and told him how smooth the sting went.

Jim Jones said, "Our sting went just as smooth."

MD said, "Man, it was just like that vision you had when we were praying."

Jim Jones said, "That's a trip, ain't it?"

MD responded, "Yeah, for real. The IA agents are on their way up to the church with those task force officers."

Jim Jones said, "That's where we all are right now."

MD said, "We are on our way up there too."

By the time the Bloods got there, Me-Ma and Mommu were just getting there too. MD, D-Rock, Jim Jones, and O. G. Van all walked up to Me-Ma and Mommu and hugged them.

Me-Ma and Mommu said that they had something very important to ask the Crips and the Bloods, so everyone went into the church.

The lieutenant of the IA agents told his agents to keep an eye on the officers in the van so he could hear what Me-Ma and Mommu had to say.

The church was filled with Crips and Bloods. Me-Ma and Mommu walked up to the podium and told everyone to sit because they need everyone's full attention. Even the IA lieutenant's attention was needed for what they were about to ask. No one knew what they were about to ask, not even the pastors or chaplains knew.

Me-Ma asked O. G. Van, Jim Jones, MD, and D-Rock to please come up on the podium. The four young men went up onto the podium, wondering what was about to happen. Everyone had their eyes on the podium, and everyone could feel the Holy Spirit shooting up in their bones.

Me-Ma looked at the four Crips and Bloods and said, "God loves all of you Crips and Bloods, as you well know by now. Jim Jones, I know that you know because it was you that He gave this vision to, and it came pass just as He gave it to you. So can I see a raise of hands from those of you who know that God ain't no joke?"

Everyone raised their hands. She continued, "Can I see a raise of hands from everyone who knows that God has forgiven them of all of their sins?"

As she said that, she turned around and looked right at MD and O. G. Van (the shooters of her and Mommu's children), the two who had been forgiven much themselves. Everyone in the church raised their hands again. She continued, "Remember that you all raised your hands to those questions."

Meanwhile, the task force officers were still out in the parking lot in the vans, handcuffed with blue and red rags around their necks, not knowing what was going on. But they did know that they were in a church's parking lot.

The demons that were assigned to the task force officers were in the atmosphere right outside of the church's parking lot, and God's angels were also in the atmosphere, but they were right in side of the church's parking lot, not allowing those demons near the officers for a mighty move of God was about to take place. The task force officers were just sitting still, not speaking because they did not know if the van was bugged.

Me-Ma continued, "Now that you've all admitted that God is all powerful and that He has forgiven you all. God wants you all to show that same compassion and forgiveness to those officers out there in those vans, handcuffed."

As she said those words, she was looking at the IA lieutenant who had the authority to let those officers go. The lieutenant was a Christian too, so he knew that Me-Ma and Mommu were being led by the Holy Spirit.

Me-Ma continued, "If you want God to forgive you, you have to forgive those who have wronged you."

The pastors and the chaplains looked at each other and just smiled because they knew that God was doing a mightier work than they thought He was going to do with this situation.

Me-Ma said, "So now again, I asked you all to raise your hands if you are willing to forgive those officers who were going to shoot blank bullets over your heads, knowing that God has forgiven you all even though y'all were shooting real bullets right at each other. Can you now, knowing how much God has forgiven you, forgive those officers?"

MD and O. G. Van (the actual shooters of the children, who had been forgiven) raised their hands first, then slowly, the rest of the Crips and Bloods raised their hands.

The lieutenant and the chaplains and pastors were the last ones to raise their hands.

Me-Ma asked the lieutenant, "Can we go out to the vans and let those officers know that the Crips and Bloods forgive them? And can you please release them right in front of us?"

The lieutenant said, "Yes, we can."

The lieutenant and the police chaplains led Me-Ma and Mommu out of the church first, then the Crips and the Bloods followed them with the pastors bringing up the rear. When they got to the vans, the Crips and the Bloods surrounded the vehicles.

The lieutenant told the IA agents what was going on, and they were shocked that the lieutenant had agreed to release the officers with no charges. The IA agents opened up all four van doors and told the officers to step out.

The officers all piled out, and they stood together, handcuffed with blue and red rags around their necks. When the officers saw that they were surrounded by Crips and Bloods and the agents started uncuffing them, they thought that the IA agents were going to allow the Crips and the Bloods to beat them.

The lieutenant told the officers' chaplains to explain what was going on. The chaplain from the Altadena sheriff station walked toward the task force officers, then the chaplain from the Pasadena police station walked over with him. As they got right in front of their own station officers, the Pasadena chaplain said, "Today is your blessed day. I would say lucky day, but there is no such thing as luck. You're either blessed or you're not."

The sergeant of the task force officers said, "What are you talking about, preacher?"

The chaplain said, "You still want to be hard, huh? Listen, I'm going to let you decide the next steps you and your officers will take. Me and the Pasadena police chaplain overheard your whole plan of attack against the Crips and the Bloods. He was in the locker room listening, and I was in the locker room listening. Only God could have placed us there right at those moments and not let y'all know that we were there."

The sergeant said, "So that's how the IA found out."

The chaplain said, "You will not believe how we were led to the IA, but I'm going to let you hear from the Crip himself, whom the Lord showed in a vision how to stop y'all from shooting at them." The chaplain called Jim Jones over to him and told him to finish the story.

Jim Jones said, "The chaplains and the pastors came to us and told us what y'all had planned, so we prayed for the wisdom on how to stop your plan. While we were praying, the Lord gave me a vision of a car load of four heads coming down our street about to do a drive-by, but in that same vision, a van came up behind the car load and pulled it over and, at gunpoint, had all of the task force officers out of their car, face down on the ground. I saw IA on the jackets of those who pulled over. After the prayer, I told the chaplains of that vision that God gave me during the prayer, and they knew that that was God's answer to our prayer. I did not even know what IA was, but the chaplains knew, and now that vision has come to pass right before our eyes."

The sergeant of the task force officers said, "So you want us to believe that God set us up?"

Jim Jones said, "No, I want you to believe that Satan set you up, but God delivered you, just like He delivered us Crips and Bloods from Satan's set up."

Tears started rolling down Jim Jones's face, and when all of the Crips and Bloods saw his tears, they all (about 250 of them) moved in closer to him to show him strength as one body. Jim Jones continued talking to the officers, "Just like God has forgiven us Crips and Bloods for much, we forgive you officers for the least of your attacks on us."

Me-Ma and Mommu walked through the Crips and Bloods, as MD and O. G. Van walked with them, holding their hands. When they got to Jim Jones, they hugged him and told him, "That message was straight from God, son."

Jim Jones said, "I know because I could not have thought of those words to say myself."

Me-Ma said, "His thoughts are higher than your thoughts."

She smiled at Jim Jones and turned to the officers and said, "Now, you listen to what Mommu and I have to say. We are the mothers of those two children that were shot and sent to heaven. We rather let our kids be in heaven right now instead of here on this earth. Since we are at peace and understand the spiritual aspects of life and death and have submitted it all to God, the Lord has blessed us with all of these Crips and Bloods as our spiritual children. We forgive them and love them, and we want you officers to stop looking for the shooters of our children. Our children are in heaven, right where we want them. As far as the shooters are concerned, they do not exist anymore. All of these gentlemen are born-again Christians, and their past has been done away with as if it never happened. Now, thank you for listening, and we also want you officers to know that we love you too and that God wants all of you to give Him your Lives."

There were sixteen task force officers there, and they did not even notice that they still had on the red and blue rags around their necks.

The lieutenant of the IA agents told the task force officers, "Because of the Crips and Bloods forgiven you all, we are not filing charges against you, and we suggest that you take those cars back to the impound, but we will be destroying your extra weapons that we took off from y'all."

Jim Jones, M.D. asked the I.A. agents if they could ask the task-force officers a question. Mommu was standing right next to Jim Jones as he asked the officers to please come to their barbecue the next day at Loma Alta Park.

The officers were still feeling out of place and trying to act hard. Mommu said, "That's the least you officers can do after these young men have forgiven you all without y'all even asking to be forgiven. You have not even apologized to these Crips and Bloods."

The sergeant of the officers looked at his men, and they shook their heads yes. The sergeant asked Jim Jones, "What time should we show up?"

Jim Jones smiled and said, "We need help setting up, so let's say around 9:00 a.m."

The lieutenant said, "See, instead of eating prison food in the morning, you officers will be setting up a barbecue at a park."

The sergeant huddled up with his officers, who were just forgiven and also invited to a feast by the ones they were trying to wrong. He told his officers, "There are not the same Crips and Bloods that used to put fear in their hoods."

One of the officers said that they need to apologize to them and to their station chaplains. The sergeant agreed, and he came out of the huddle and asked if he could say something to everyone.

Everyone gathered around the sixteen officers, all of the Crips and the Bloods (about three hundred of them), plus the pastors and the chaplains. Me-Ma and Mommu turned to the sergeant as he said, "We all apologize to you Crips and Bloods, and we sincerely thank you for your forgiveness. And to our station chaplains, we also apologize. Please forgive us. And to the IA agents, we also apologize and thank you for not locking us up, as you surely could have."

The sergeant looked at Me-Ma and Mommu and said, "You two women are the ones that lost your children, right?"

They both nodded their heads yes.

And he asked, "You have forgiven the Crips and Bloods for killing them?"

Me-Ma said, "The devil wants y'all to think that they were killed. Our children are in heaven with God and Jesus Christ."

Mommu also said, "Just think about the power of forgiveness. Here we are, the mothers of the children that have been sent to heaven, the Crips and the Bloods who were misused to fire their guns that sent our children to heaven, the officers who would be chasing the Crips and Bloods as they continue to shoot at each other in retaliation after retaliation, the pastors and the chaplains who would be holding funerals and condolence meetings, but instead of all that evil taking place, we are under the power of forgiveness which sets us free from the attacks of the enemy, which is Satan and his demons. We are at peace knowing that God is in the details."

The sergeant said, "When you break it down like that, it really starts to make sense."

The lieutenant said, "God is really awesome." He told the sergeant that he and his men could leave, and he hoped to see them at the barbecue. The lieutenant also told the task force officers that their buddy who worked at the impound would be released with no charges.

The sergeant said, "We really do appreciate everything that has taken place here this evening, and we will be at the barbecue tomorrow."

The chaplains and the pastors got together while they had everybody there and decided to just have one big barbecue instead of two of them separate from each other. So it was agreed that the barbecue would be held as one instead of two. It would be held the next day, which was Saturday, so everyone would have Sunday off for church. All of the Crips and the Bloods and the church members from both

Altadena and Pasadena, plus the IA agents and chaplains, as well as the task force officers would all be at this barbecue fellowship, eating, playing sports, and just getting to know each other.

Mommu and Me-Ma were so excited and blessed to be a part of what God was doing. He just kept blowing their minds.

The task force officers all took their cars back to the impound where they got them from. By the time they got there, their friend who gave them the cars illegally had been released by the IA agents. When he saw the officers, he was a bit upset at how things went down and he told them so.

The officers let him get it off his chest, and when he finished speaking and cussing them out for putting his career on the line, the officers told him that they were very sorry and that it would never happen again. The sergeant of the task force officers asked him if he could find it in his heart to forgive them.

The impound worker was not ready for that question neither did the sergeant's officers expect him to ask that question. They all looked at him and realized that tears were coming down his face.

One of the officers asked the sergeant what was wrong, and the sergeant looked at his officers and asked them if they understood the break that they were given that evening. The sergeant said, "And the only reason we got that break was because the Crips and Bloods gave it to us. The same Crips and Bloods that we were trying to turn on each other. Only God has that kind of power."

All of the officers then started realizing the depth of the forgiveness that they were given. The sergeant asked the impound worker if he could pick him up and take him to a barbecue tomorrow, and he said yes. Then they all agreed to meet up at the barbecue the next morning at 8:30 a.m. so that they could help set things up.

The sergeant said, "I never felt the peace that I'm feeling right now."

One of his officers said, "We all feel that peace since we are not in jail and still have our jobs."

The sergeant responded, "The peace that I feel is deeper than that. It's like I can see God watching over us, and I now know that we are in His care."

The rest of the officers were surprised at their sergeant's response because he was usually a hard case to deal with. The sergeant said, "I'll see you all at the barbecue in the morning," as he got in his car and left.

The rest of the officers followed suit, and they all left, thinking about what God had done for them.

Narrator

It very easily slipped the officers' minds that God was the one really looking out for them. Although it was the Crips and Bloods that forgave them, it was God who moved on them through His teaching of forgiveness through Me-Ma and Mommu. The spirit of forgiveness was softening the officers' hearts, just as it did in the Crips' and Bloods' hearts.

14

CHAPTER

The next morning at seven, the pastors from both churches met at the Altadena church. They had previously told both of their congregations to meet them there and bring any donations for the barbecue. As the congregations started showing up from Pasadena and Altadena, the parking lot overfilled, and when the police and sheriff chaplains showed up, they were amazed at the turnout. There was over three hundreds of Crips and Bloods who had not arrived yet.

The chaplains told the pastors that they would start leaking people out toward the park where the barbecue was being held. The pastors said that it was a good idea. So the chaplains started telling people to move out toward the park. It had so much food there that it was sure to be more than enough. The pastors had message and heard testimonies. The four ex-gang members that were paying for the educations of the Crips and Bloods came up to the church and told the pastors that they had all of the acceptance papers for the Crips and Bloods and that they all got accepted.

The Altadena pastor said, "That is just awesome. Let's wait to tell them at the barbecue as a surprise for them."

They all agreed to that. The pastors were just amazed at God's timing. The pastors also rented some super big barbecue pits and some professional cooks to handle all of the cooking, which would take a lot of pressure off from Me-Ma and Mommu, who wanted to do all of the cooking. They did not anticipate doing both of the barbecues on one day.

The task force chaplains hired a camera crew to film the whole barbecue too. So they all drove up to the park, and as they got to the first stoplight, the task force officers pulled up behind them. Then when they got to the next stoplight, the IA agents pulled up behind the officers.

Everyone started blowing their car horns in realizing each other's presence. As they drove up the hill blowing their horns, the Crips and Bloods were across the street, and they heard the horns first. When they saw who it was, they drove in behind them, blowing their horns too.

It was about seventy-five cars following each other, blowing their horns. It was like the procession of a funeral and a wedding, which was what it was symbolically—the dying to self of the Crips and Bloods, as well as they're now being the bride of Christ.

When they pulled into the parking lot of the park, they got out of their cars and started hugging each other. The task force officers were surprised when a few of the Crips and Bloods came over to hug them. When the sergeant felt the hug of one of the Crips, he felt the sincerity of it, and it touched him deeply enough that he looked the Crip in his eyes and said, "Thank you."

The pastors and the chaplains were again amazed at God's timing—how He had them all at the stoplights together and across streets so that they could follow each other.

Everything was set up except for the DJ's equipment. He set up his equipment with the help of the task force officers carrying up his big speakers. While the food was cooking, the pastor of the Altadena church grabbed the microphone and called for everyone's attention. Everyone quieted down, and the pastor said, "We want to open this up with a prayer of thanks to God for this special blessed day."

As the pastor prayed, the DJ put on some Juanita Bynum. It was her anointed song called "Morning Glory." After he got through praying, he asked if anyone had any testimonies that they wanted to share.

Jim Jones raised his hand, and the pastor called him up. Jim Jones grabbed the mic and looked out to the big crowd of Crips and Bloods and two congregations, plus the officers and the IA agents and said, "God is revealing Himself more and more every day, and I realize that even though we are born-again men of God [speaking of the Crips and Bloods], we still dress the same, and some of us still carry our blue and red rags [gang colors]."

The Lord was really moving on Jim Jones as he continued, "Right now, this moment, the Lord is giving me a word of knowledge. I did not plan this speech nor have I ever heard these words that He is speaking through me. So please know that it's God speaking, not me. God says it's not about putting new Crips and Bloods in these clothes.

"You cannot say that you do not feel Him or hear Him. We must renew our minds about the blue and red rags. We must renew our minds about the words *crip*, *cuz*, and *blood*. I am telling you all that this is God speaking for I could never have thought of these words myself.

"You all remember the vision He gave me about the IA busting the task force, and it came to pass as such? So please know that He is giving me these words right now. The blue rags and the clothing that we Crips wear represents the heavens above. The red rags and clothing that the Bloods wear represents the blood of the Lamb. You see, now we must put these meanings in our minds. As a matter of fact, the Lord has just given me a new meaning for each letter in the words *crips* and *bloods*.

"God just showed it to me in my mind's eye. I saw the letter *C* is for *Christians*, the letter *R* is for *riding*, the letter *I* is for *in*, the letter *P* is for *peace*, and the letter *S* is for *salvation*. So we have Christians riding in peace and salvation. For the word *blood*, I saw the letter *B* as *believers*, the letter *L* as *living*, the letter *O* as *off*, the next *O* as *of*, the *D* as *deliverance*, and the *S* as *salvation*. Thus, we have believers living off of deliverance and salvation. Can we all agree on that?"

All the Crips and Bloods started waving their blue and red rags in the air. The Crips were hollering, "From the heavens above, heavens above." While the Bloods were hollering, "Blood of the Lamb, blood of the Lamb." They did that for about five times, back to back.

As the Crips and Bloods started waving their red and blue rags in the air, hollering their new claim, the angels were flying above them in the atmosphere. It was one angel for each Crip and each Blood, just as there was one angel for each task force officer and IA agent. Each angel hovered right above their assigned soul, and all at the same time, they blew God's anointing Spirit on each one of them, and each individual fell backward off on their feet. They were all on the ground shaking for five seconds or so, and just as suddenly as they started shaking, they stopped, and the angels went higher into the atmosphere.

The pastor grabbed the microphone and said, "That was the Holy Spirit coming into each one of you."

While the pastor was talking, the Crips and the Bloods were speaking in tongues, and tears were coming down their faces.

The task force officers and the IA agents all walked up to where the pastor was talking. The Spirit of the Lord was moving rapidly throughout everyone there, and the pastor knew that those officers and IA agents wanted to confess Jesus as Lord of their lives. So without them even asking, the pastor led them in prayer to receive Jesus Christ as Lord of their lives.

As soon as they said, "In Jesus's name, amen!" the angels in the air started dancing and rejoicing, and the demons flew away to hide from Satan because they had lost the task force officers and the IA agents.

The pastor said, "Praise God, Almighty, let's eat, rejoice, and be merry."

As they all ate and played ball and were fellowshipping down on earth, the angels saw Satan beating on his demons and chasing them because they had lost the souls of the Crips, Bloods, IA agents, and the task force officers. The angels grieved for their fallen brothers because they knew that there was nothing that they could do to help them because the fallen angels (demons) had made their choice of whom they wanted to serve when they left heaven with Satan. Nevertheless, the angels were grieved for their fallen brothers.

*****

After a couple of hours of playing sports, eating, and fellowshipping, the pastor called up the four gentlemen that were paying for the Crips' and Bloods' trade tech schooling so they could pass out everyone's acceptance papers. The pastor called for everyone's attention. He reintroduced Young Q., Dub, T. Moses, and Donovan (Nitty). Everyone remembered them except for the officers and the IA agents, who were informed about those four ex-gang members financing the Crips and Bloods to go to a trade tech school.

T. Moses grabbed the microphone from the pastor and said, "We have everyone's acceptance papers, and no one was denied. As I call your names, you can come up and get your envelope that will also have your class schedules in it and a voucher that will cover any books that you may have to get while at school."

As T. Moses called out their names, they all started walking up to get their envelopes from Dub, Young Q., and Nitty. It looked like a graduation or something. After they passed them all out, the pastor said that there was someone else he wanted to introduce to everyone.

The pastor said, "Please give a round of applause to the gentleman that also used to live the gangsta lifestyle, went to prison, gave his life to the Lord, and now he is an ordained minister. He has the most proper rap song that God has given him, and he wishes to lay it down for you all right now. His name is Brother Timothy Ross. Some of us know him as Two-Step. The name of the song is 'We Got Teach.'"

Two-Step grabbed the microphone, and the DJ put the beat down for him, and the words flowed from Two-Step like running water.

Everyone was feeling him and bumping to the beat. MD and Jim Jones felt that they should pray for all of the other gangs out there that have not received the blessing that they just received. They wanted to pray for the Southern Mexicans and Northern Mexicans for they were at war with each other, just as hard as the Crips and Bloods were out there. Jim Jones and MD also wanted to pray for the White Aryan Brothers and the Asian gangs too. Plus, they wanted to pray for the rest of the Crips and Bloods gangs out there that were still banging.

Jim Jones and MD knew that if they could be saved, so could the rest of those bangers out there. So Jim Jones, MD, O. G. Van, and D-Rock walked up to the pastor, as Two-Step finished his rap song, and told the pastor about what they wanted to pray for.

Me-Ma and Mommu were sitting next to the pastor, and they heard what their boys wanted to pray about, and they just looked at each other and smiled.

The pastor gave the microphone to MD, and MD gave it to Jim Jones and said, "You say the prayer, my brother."

Jim Jones grabbed the microphone and asked for everyone's attention. Everyone looked up to where he was standing as he said, "The Lord has put it upon us to pray for the rest of those out there that are still gangbanging. For those out there that are still misuse by Satan, like we were. As a matter of fact, the Lord has just revealed to me right this moment that Satan is really going to be attacking them because he knows that he lost us, and he does not want to lose them. So we need to be standing in the gap for I'm no preacher, so y'all know that God has just given me that word."

Jim Jones turned to the camera man that was filming the while picnic and told him, "Make sure that you get a picture of all of these Crips and Bloods bowing our heads in prayer for all gangbangers to repent and return to the Lord."

The camera man had already put the whole barbecue on film. He had about five cameras strategically placed throughout the park so that he would not miss a thing.

So on the film, he had the Crips and Bloods, the task force officers and agents falling out under the power of the Holy Spirit. The officers and agents accepted Jesus Christ as Lord of their lives. Also, he had the Crips and Bloods new meaning of their gang names (CRIPS and BLOODS) and how Bloods now means blood of the Lamb and the blue of the Crips representing the heavens above. The camera man told Jim Jones, "I have everything that has went down here today on camera."

The chaplains of the sheriff and police stations said that they had access to the media, and they would more than likely be on the news because they were going to send copies of that film to all the news channels that they could.

Jim Jones said, "Well, let us pray then because I feel God boiling up inside of me."

All of the Crips and Bloods hollered, "Let's do this."

Jim Jones reached out his hand to MD, D-Rock grabbed MD's other hand, and O. G. Van grabbed D-Rock's other hand. All of the rest of the Crips and Bloods plus the two churches all grabbed hands so that they would all be in one accord. As Jim Jones started praying, all of the church members started praying in tongues, so as not to drown out Jim Jones's prayer.

"Lord God, Almighty, the brothers and sisters and I come to You in one accord in prayer and supplication on behalf of those gang-bangers out there in society who do not know that they are being misused by Satan. We know that we are now Your children and that the blood of Your Son cleansed us and made us righteous. So we know that Your ears are open to hear our prayers. We also know that You are against those that do evil.

"Father God, we stand in the gap for those gangbangers that do not know that they are being tossed to-and-fro by the enemy. We pray that they see this film on the news and be moved by Your Spirit, as we were and are still being moved upon. We also pray that laborers be sent their way, as You sent laborers our way, that would show them Your mercy, grace, deliverance, and forgiveness that You have shown to us through Your laborers.

"We thank You for softening the hearts of the task force officers and the IA agents, as well as softening our hearts, Father God. So we know and believe that those other gangbangers out there can have their hearts softened too. We also thank You for Me-Ma and Mommu for their sincere love for us and their true forgiveness. We love You, Father. In Jesus's name, amen!"

The big crowd all said amen together. What a beautiful sound.

Jim Jones looked at the pastors and said, "I never knew what God was going to pray through me. I was not even in my body during that prayer. God had me suspended in the air, watching the whole scene, as He prayed through me."

Tears were flowing down his face as he told the pastors what he had just experienced.

The pastor from the Altadena church told Jim Jones, "God is going to do mighty things through you."

Jim Jones said, "I receive that."

The pastor gave the microphone to Brother Two-Step, and he rocked the whole park with a few more of his Gospel rap songs, and he also gave a brief testimony of how he came to know the Lord, Jesus Christ, while he was in prison. Two-Step testified that in prison was where God gave him all of those rap songs that he was singing.

Narrator

The Lord Jesus Christ came and paid for everyone's sins—gang-bangers, homosexuals, robbers, killers, sexual predators, dope users, dope dealers, Blacks, Whites, Mexicans, Asians, and everyone else that exist here on earth. All one must do is to confess with their mouths and believe in their hearts that Jesus Christ is the Lord and that no matter what they have done in their past, God will cleanse them from all unrighteousness and change them and their ways.

We cannot change ourselves. Just come as you are, and God will change ourselves. God will change you by His Spirit. We, as a church, need to take the Word of God to the streets, just as Jesus Christ came down from heaven and brought Himself to us. We must take God's love to the people out there who cannot find their way to heaven without Jesus Christ coming to us, so it is with the people out there in the streets that cannot seem to find their way to church. So we must take the church to them. God bless us all. Amen!

The Alpha and Omega, the beginning, and the ending. (Revelation 1:3)

ABOUT THE AUTHOR

Brother Cavin O'Ferral was born again on September 15, 1997 in the hole at Wasco State Prison in California. He was sentenced under California's "Three strikes and you're out" law, which calls for twenty-five years to life sentence for any third felony conviction (nonviolent/nonserious or violent/serious). Brother Cavin O'Ferral had been arrested for a possession of ten dollars' worth of rock cocaine in his pocket on January 1, 1995. He had previously been arrested for robberies and burglaries for which he served his time for.

He is a father of 7 grown kids and grandfather of 13 grandchildren.

He is an ex-gang member from the Altadena Blocc Crips, and his gang name was Jim Jones, which are both used in the book "His Vision". The Lord had California's "Three strikes and you're out" law revised by the voters and Brother Cain O'Ferral was released from prison.

He is 57 years old and will continue to work toward bringing all gangbangers to the Lord.

He has never been to college. He received his GED at Soledad prison in 1990. He gives God all the glory for writing this book through him.

CPSIA information can be obtained
at www.ICGtesting.com
Printed in the USA
LVHW110144140821
695160LV00004B/425